WE HOLD
THESE
TRUTHS

WE HOLD THESE TRUTHS

From Magna Carta
to the Bill of Rights

JAMES AYARS

THE VIKING PRESS   NEW YORK

First Edition
Copyright © James Ayars, 1977
All rights reserved
First published in 1977 by The Viking Press
625 Madison Avenue, New York, N.Y. 10022
Published simultaneously in Canada by
Penguin Books Canada Limited
Printed in U.S.A.
1 2 3 4 5 81 80 79 78 77

Library of Congress Cataloging in Publication Data
Ayars, James Sterling. We hold these truths.
Includes index.
Summary: A brief history of the ideas of liberty and
equality with sketches of the lives of Stephen Langton,
John Lilburne, and George Mason, who contributed to the
preservation and development of these ideas.
1. Civil rights—Great Britain—History—Juvenile
literature. 2. Civil rights—United States—History—
Juvenile literature. [1. Civil rights—History] I. Title.
JC599.G7A93   323.4'09   77-2799
ISBN 0-670-75392-0

In memory of my great-grandfather,
HARVEY BOSTWICK HURD,
abolitionist, self-educated attorney,
friend of John Brown and Abraham Lincoln,
juvenile court pioneer, codifier of state statutes,
university law school professor,
and advocate of justice for all

CONTENTS

PREFACE

Most citizens of the United States learn during their school days that their country was at one time "a new nation, conceived in liberty and dedicated to the proposition that all men are created equal."

The nation to which Abraham Lincoln referred in his Gettysburg Address had been brought forth only fourscore and seven years earlier, but most of the ideals of liberty and equality, the self-evident truths, and the inalienable rights on which it was founded had been long established. These had been kept alive over many years by brave and dedicated men and women who refused to let them die. At a fortunate time in history these truths and rights came together to conceive and give birth to the new nation of which Lincoln spoke at Gettysburg.

The introductory chapter of this book gives a brief history of the most important ideas of liberty and equality, the truths that by 1776 were held to be self-evident and the rights that were believed to be inalienable. Each of the three chapters following the first one sketches the life of a man who, by his wise efforts and heroic sacrifices, contributed mightily to the preservation and development of these truths and these rights.

Stephen Langton, born in England about eight centuries ago, was more than any other man responsible for Magna Carta, the great English document on which many American Revolutionary heroes based their arguments for freedom from royal tyranny. John Lilburne, who lived in the England of Charles I and Oliver Cromwell, fought the tyranny of Parliament and the lord protector as well as of the king—most notably for freedom of speech and of the press. George Mason, American Revolutionary, in writing the Virginia Declaration of Rights, brought together where they could be read the rights for which men and women had struggled and sacrificed over the centuries. Although Mason helped to write the Constitution, he refused to sign it because it did not contain a bill of rights; indirectly he forced the new nation to make its first ten amendments *the* Bill of Rights.

The new nation of which Lincoln spoke could be "conceived in liberty and dedicated to the proposition that all men are created equal" only because of idealistic, courageous individuals—women as well as men—like Langton, Lilburne, and Mason. Bygone ages have had them. The present needs them.

James Ayars

ONE

Where the Truths Came From

When the solemn delegates from thirteen of the British colonies in North America had sweated through their historic meetings at Philadelphia in the hot summer of 1776, the truths they proclaimed in their Declaration of Independence were not new. The nation they were founding was new. But the truths on which they justified its founding were centuries old.

"We hold these Truths to be self-evident," they reminded British King George III and the rest of the world, "that all Men are created equal, that they are endowed by their Creator with certain unalienable Rights, that among these are Life, Liberty, and the Pursuit of Happiness. . . ."

These truths and the ideals and legal customs written thirteen years later into the first ten amendments to the United States Constitution had been a long time evolving. They were accepted, even demanded, by Englishmen living in England—at least for themselves.

Most people in the thirteen colonies that became the United States were descended from men and women who had come from England. Until 1775 or 1776 many of them had thought of themselves as Englishmen, with all the legal rights and privileges of Englishmen. Many of those without English backgrounds had become infected with English ideas about the inherent rights of individuals and the limited rights of kings and parliaments.

Time and again, men who spoke for the colonists before 1776 referred to Magna Carta, the great charter to which the English King John, facing armed and rebellious subjects "on the meadow which is called Runnymede," grudgingly acceded on a June day in 1215. And they referred not only to Magna Carta but to interpretations of it by English judges who had, in effect, expanded the rights to which Englishmen were entitled by the common law, the unwritten, widely accepted legal customs of the nation.

Probably few of the American colonists knew that some of the basic ideas in Magna Carta were centuries older than the great charter itself. They may not have known of the ancient witan or witenagemot, the "meeting of the wise," a type of legal assembly that the Angles, Saxons, and Jutes had brought with them from mainland Europe when they crossed the North Sea into Britain. The witan closely represented the free men of the tribe or nation (but not the slaves or near-slaves). It served as adviser to the king and could take a direct part in any act of government. It had the power to elect a king or to dethrone a king—and did.

The invasions of England by the Danes, which began in 787, did not destroy the witan. Edward the Confessor, the revered king who died only a few months before the Norman invasion of 1066, had been elected by the witan in preference to a candidate who by royal inheritance had a stronger claim to the English throne.

The witan, as an institution, died soon after William the Conqueror, the leader of the Norman invasion, had cowed its panicky members into electing him king of the English at Westminster Abbey in London on Chrismas Day, 1066. It was succeeded by the Curia Regis, the court of the king's feudal vassals, and later by Parliament. But many of the traditions of the witan lived on and kept the English kings, even the most powerful ones, from establishing absolute monarchies.

Most of the leaders in the thirteen rebellious colonies were aware that Magna Carta had established in writing that the king himself, like all other men, was not above the law. They knew the fate of certain kings who had mistakenly believed they could ignore or defy the laws of the realm—the laws passed by Parliament or the laws well established by custom (common law). They remembered that one of those kings, Charles I, had lost his head on the executioner's block after a violent revolution and that another, James II, had lost his kingdom after fleeing to France during a mild uprising often called the Glorious Revolution.

The men who wrote and signed the American Declaration of Independence knew that several of their colonial charters from British kings and some of the laws passed by colonial legislatures contained references to Magna Carta and to Sir Edward Coke, a famous English judge. The decisions and writings of Coke on Magna Carta and the common law had had the effect of increasing the rights of individuals.

In the Body of Liberties of 1641, the earliest legislation

[*3*]

passed in the Massachusetts Colony, several sections were derived from Magna Carta, the first two from chapters thirty-nine and forty.

> 1. No mans life shall be taken away, no mans honour or good name shall be stayned, no mans person shall be arested, restrayned, banished, dismembred, nor any wayes punished . . . unlesse it be by vertue or equitie of some expresse law of the Country. . . .
>
> 2. Every person within this Jurisdiction, whether Inhabitant or forreiner shall enjoy the same justice and law, that is generall for the plantation, which we constitute and execute one towards another without partialitie or delay.

The example set in the Massachusetts Body of Liberties was followed in the New Haven Code, 1656; the Charter of Fundamental Liberties of West New Jersey, 1677; the New York Charter of Liberties, 1683; the South Carolina Act, 1712; and the North Carolina Act, 1715.

The Rhode Island charter of 1663, at the insistence of Roger Williams, contained a reference to chapter thirty-nine of Magna Carta. The wording of the Pennsylvania Charter of Privileges of 1682 showed William Penn's familiarity with Magna Carta and its interpretations by Sir Edward Coke. In a pamphlet he issued in 1675, *England's Present Interest,* Penn asserted the rights of the colonists as Englishmen to be protected by Magna Carta as interpreted by Coke.

At first the colonists were concerned with protecting themselves against the king. Later, they decided they should protect themselves against Parliament also. They adopted Coke's idea of the supremacy of the common law over Parliament as well as over the king. A pamphlet published in Boston in 1689 was a defense of the colonists' claim to the rights of Englishmen by appeal to their colonial charter, to Magna Carta, and to common law.

In 1735, forty years before the shooting began at Lexington and Concord, Andrew Hamilton defended printer John Peter Zenger's right to freedom of the press, basing his arguments on Coke and Magna Carta. In 1765 Thomas Hutchinson, in a speech on the Stamp Act that the English Parliament had imposed on the colonists, said that the act was "against Magna Carta and the natural rights of Englishmen . . . [and], according to Lord Coke, null and void."

MAGNA CARTA NOT A ONE-TIME THING

What was, or is, Magna Carta, this great charter that American colonists seeking freedom referred to again and again?

Under glass in the British Museum, London, one of the "original" copies can be seen today—a large sheet of yellowed vellum almost covered with Latin words written in characters that look strange to modern eyes. It is dated June 15, in the seventeenth year of the reign of King John (1215). Three other "original" copies exist. All are in England. Two of the four copies are in the British Museum; one is in the cathedral at Salisbury and one in the cathedral at Lincoln. The one at Lincoln is considered the best. It is 18¼ inches long and 17¾ inches wide.

Magna Carta was, and is, more than a large sheet of vellum almost covered with Latin words. It climaxed a rebellion against their king by many of the English barons and other nobles. It was a royal grant giving back to the nobles—and some of the common people, too—certain rights they believed they had lost. Closely associated with it was Stephen Langton, archbishop of Canterbury, as well as John Lackland, then king of England. It was, and is, a document containing ideas and ideals that have echoed and re-echoed down through more than seven and a half centuries in the history of freedom-loving English-speaking peoples.

Like the American Declaration of Independence and the so-called Bill of Rights (the first ten amendments to the Constitution of the United States), Magna Carta promises rights and privileges that free men (not serfs) had previously enjoyed—rights and privileges they had lost or were losing under a stubborn, willful ruler.

In its sixty-three short chapters, or *capitula,* Magna Carta is a mixture of many matters. Some of the chapters refer to matters that were very important to the English people of 1215 but are of little interest today: for example, that fish weirs should be removed from the Thames and Medway rivers, that no widow should be compelled to marry so long as she wished to live without a husband, that "all alien knights, crossbowmen, sergeants, and mercenary soldiers" who had "come with horses and arms to the hurt of the realm" should be removed from the kingdom.

A number of the chapters refer to basic human rights— rights that are as essential today as in 1215. The meaning of the total document is that no man, not even the king, is above the law. Like all other men, the ruler must obey the law of the land.

With alterations and deletions, the charter was reissued in 1216 and again in 1217 by the regent, the aged William Marshal, the earl of Pembroke. The regent was acting for King Henry III, who, at the age of nine, had succeeded his father, King John. Marshal had long been a faithful follower of John.

With still more alterations and deletions the charter was reissued in 1225 by Henry himself, who had recently been declared of age and therefore legally able to rule the kingdom.

[6]

Probably the 1215 charter is the most important historically, the 1225 charter the most important legally.

For several years the status of Magna Carta seemed uncertain. However, in a letter written in August 1234 the king emphasized that the charter had been granted to both great and small.

In the reissues of Magna Carta, the terms *homo*, "man," and *liber homo*, "free man," were kept as in the original. Chapters involving basic human rights were retained, for example, chapters thirty-nine and forty. The substance of chapter forty of the 1215 charter was repeated in chapter twenty-nine of the 1225 version and in the same words: "*Nulli vendemus, nulli negabimus aut differemus rectum vel justiciam*" ("To no one will we sell, to no one deny or delay right or justice")—a declaration as good for today as for 1215 or 1225.

With time the acceptance and influence of Magna Carta grew. It ceased to be regarded merely as a charter forced on an unjust, unpopular king by rebellious barons and other nobles. It became a basic part of the law of the land.

Rights originally applied to "freemen" were eventually applied to all men—and now are being applied to women. As social and economic conditions changed through the centuries, interpretations of Magna Carta were adapted to meet the current legal or political needs of men who were free or wanted to be free. As English scholars, lawyers, and judges studied the charter and became acquainted with the writings of Aristotle, Thomas Aquinas, and other ancient, medieval, and later philosophers of Greece, Italy, France, and Germany, interpretations of the charter broadened.

New terms, *natural law, natural rights* (that is, the rights due a person simply because he or she was born a person), were

[7]

read into the meaning of the charter. Some of these became "unalienable rights," rights not to be surrendered.

At various times since 1215 the people who inherited Magna Carta have had to remind their heads of state, as the barons did at Runnymede, that no ruler is above the law. They have had to reassert as a self-evident truth that all individuals are born with certain inalienable rights no government, no head of state, can take from them—that Magna Carta is not a one-time thing.

THE SELF-EVIDENT TRUTHS

When Thomas Jefferson wrote the Declaration of Independence, he mentioned only two self-evident truths: (1) "that all Men are created equal," and (2) "that they are endowed by their Creator with certain unalienable Rights."

Events that preceded and followed the signing and sealing of Magna Carta had helped to establish the truth that all men are created equal—at least that all men, including the king, are subject to law and, ideally, equal before the law. To help this truth remain established, American colonial leaders at the end of the Revolutionary War proposed a federal constitution—an agreement among the states.

At least one federal constitution had existed on the North American continent for several centuries. Even before the time of Christopher Columbus the Iroquois and related Indian tribes had their Great Binding Law of the Five Nations, a federal constitution that provided for equal voting rights, set up the ideal that government officials should be responsible to the people who elected them, and recognized the obligation of each present generation to future generations. The white conquerors of the Iroquois should have a constitution that provided no less.

Jefferson named only three "unalienable rights" in the Declaration of Independence: "Life, Liberty, and the Pursuit of Happiness." But he implied others. Three named by John Locke, an English philosopher much read by American colonial leaders, were life, liberty, and property.

The "Pursuit of Happiness" Jefferson may have borrowed from his friend George Mason, who had written the Virginia Declaration of Rights late in May 1776. A paragraph in Mason's first draft of the Declaration: "That all Men are born equally free and independent, and have certain inherent natural Rights, of which they can not by any Compact, deprive or divest their Posterity; among which are the Enjoyment of Life and Liberty, with the Means of acquiring and possessing Property, and pursueing and obtaining Happiness and Safety."

Other rights that had become inalienable to Americans by 1776, though not mentioned in the Declaration of Independence, are provided for in the Constitution or in the first ten amendments.

One of these rights was a government that would insure legal justice. Over many centuries Englishmen had come to believe that such a government must consist of three separate branches: legislative, executive, judicial. John Locke, in his *Two Treatises of Government,* in 1689 traced the development of these three branches of government from man in a state of nature to man who, for his safety, has entered a state of society.

Jefferson and other colonial leaders not only knew the writings of Locke. They knew English history. They knew that any English king who had tried to be lawmaker and judge, as well as executive (three in one), had become tyrannical. They realized that their best chances for legal justice lay with a government of three separate branches. And so the Constitution itself provides for legislative, executive, and judicial branches, each separate from the others and each having specifically designated duties and powers.

Perhaps the most precious human rights are protected by the first ten amendments, or Bill of Rights. Between the signing and sealing of Magna Carta in 1215 and ratification of these amendments in 1791, many thoughts were thought, much history happened, and many persons suffered for their thoughts and acts of conscience. For helping the English people, through Magna Carta, recover some of the rights that had been theirs, Stephen Langton incurred the powerful displeasure of a king and a pope and was suspended from his high office as archbishop of Canterbury. For his part in the printing of books the government considered libelous and seditious, John Lilburne was whipped at the tail of a cart for two miles through London streets; for speaking and writing thoughts the government considered dangerous, he was confined to prison for many years. For insisting on practicing her Quaker religion in Massachusetts, Mary Dyer was hanged from a giant elm on Boston Common; one of her persecutors who saw her said, "Mary Dyer did hang as a flag for others to take example by." For publicly speaking his objections to a constitution that did not contain a bill of rights, George Mason was heckled and ridiculed by street crowds; he also lost the close friendship of an old friend, George Washington.

Stephen Langton, John Lilburne, William Penn, John Milton, Mary Dyer, Anne Hutchinson, Roger Williams, Nathaniel Bacon, John Peter Zenger, George Mason—these are among the many courageous persons who worked and suffered for human rights. The list is long. Freedom of religion, speech, and the press; security against unreasonable search and seizure; the right to a speedy and public trial—these are among the rights included in the first ten amendments to the United States Constitution. Among the most important rights in other amendments are freedom from slavery and equal voting rights for persons of all colors and both sexes.

The struggle for human rights is not ended. With the passage of time, other rights will become recognized as inalienable. Other persons will work and suffer to make them become part of the law of the land.

TWO

Stephen Langton

A scholar, a university professor, a poet, a priest, a student of the Bible, a cardinal, and an archbishop, Stephen Langton was also an adviser to a king and to his rebellious subjects. But first and always he was an Englishman—an Englishman with very definite ideas about the rights of Englishmen.

If he had not held to those ideas with wisdom, tact, and courage, the rights of Englishmen today—the rights of Americans, too—would probably be far less than they are.

Much of what Stephen Langton did as a scholar and religious leader is well known. It is solidly set down in history books of the Middle Ages. But when and where he was born, where he received his early education, are only good guesses based on patient historical sleuthing. And, because diplomacy tends to be secret, details of his part in one of the most important events in history, the writing and acceptance of Magna Carta, are not known with certainty. They can only be surmised from a knowledge of where he was when—and what happened at the time or later. At a crucial period in the history of the English people, in the history of human rights, Langton seems to have been at times only a shadowy figure, but one that moved in the center of important events.

That Stephen Langton was born in Lincolnshire, a flattish county in northern England, that his father was a Henry Langton, that he had one brother named Simon and another named Walter is certain. Also certain is that he was born near a village named Langton. But which of three villages of that name—Langton-by-Spilsby, Langton-by-Horncastle, Langton-by-Wragby—is not certain. A famous English historian, after long research, settled on Langton-by-Wragby as the probable village and on 1165 as the probable date of Stephen's birth. Of Stephen's mother he could say nothing.

Henry Langton was a country gentleman, which means that he had at least a modest amount of land and other property. Probably he lived with his family in an attractive red-brick manor house surrounded by green fields. Toward the end of his life, when his sons Stephen and Simon were out of favor with the king, Henry feared that his life was in danger. According to an old chronicler, he "left his land and goods, and for some time hid in England with a few members of his household." Later he fled to Scotland, where he died. When the king's officials heard of his flight, they confiscated his property.

The family of Henry Langton evidently had great respect

for learning and religion. Two of the sons, Stephen and Simon, went on to higher education and chose the church for their life work. All three of the sons probably had the early education typical for the sons of country gentlemen of the twelfth century.

Perhaps the Langton boys were taught by clergy of the cathedral church at Lincoln, about fifteen miles from their home. All the schools of Lincolnshire were at that time under the supervision of the head of that great church. Perhaps the boys knew and were influenced by some of the monks of the Gilbertine priory at Bullington, not far from Langton-by-Wragby. Certainly the boys studied Latin, for Stephen and Simon later read, wrote, and spoke this ancient language while performing their duties in the church.

LIFE IN PARIS

Probably at the age of fifteen or sixteen, Stephen Langton left his comfortable home in the pleasant Lincolnshire country and crossed the English Channel to France. He was on his way to Paris, the city of light, where the tree of knowledge grew.

In Paris he joined several hundred other young men who, with the distinguished scholars who were their masters, were making the University of Paris one of the most famous seats of learning for the liberal arts, theology, medicine, and law in all of Europe. At that time the great university was only in the process of becoming. The faculty was a loosely organized assemblage of masters, most of them teaching near Notre Dame, the cathedral of Our Lady, also in the process of becoming.

Before a man was allowed to teach at the university, he had to prove that he was qualified and then be licensed as a master by the chancellor of Notre Dame. A master would rent a room in the student quarters and hold classes there. An outstanding student might eventually become a master, as Stephen Langton did.

When Stephen entered the university, where he was later joined by his brother Simon, Paris occupied an island in the Seine and overflowed onto the left bank of the river. Green fields and woods could be seen beyond the gray swirl of the river as it flowed by the island. Quays stretched along part of the island shore, where vessels were moored to unload their grain, wood, and other cargoes. Not far away clustered busy shops. Most of the university students lived in crowded quarters close to the cathedral on the island or on the left bank of the river.

The period was one of excitement in the classrooms and out. Aristotle, the ancient Greek philosopher who believed that the highest function of the state was to enable its citizens to live good and happy lives, was being rediscovered. University students in England at that time have been described as "gay, ardent, and speculative." The students in Paris were like them. Although some of them wore ragged clothes and were nearly penniless, as individuals and as a group they studied and challenged the learning and ideas of the past and looked to the future.

To many of the students in Paris the future was in the church as monks, friars, or members of the secular clergy. The monks, dwelling austerely in monasteries, would contribute greatly to learning and the arts; they might become scholars, artists, writers, or recorders of history. The friars, living among the poor, lowly, and outcast, would develop a perception of the social problems of common humanity and work for reform. The secular clergy would begin their professional careers as priests among the regular church attenders; many of them would become involved in church government and a few, at suitable ages, would be named bishops. One of Stephen Langton's fellow students in Paris was an Italian, Lotario di Segni. Stephen was to know him later as Pope Innocent III.

Stephen Langton chose the secular life, the priesthood in the world, even though the quiet monastic life had some attractions for him. As a student, he had developed a deep concern for the well-being of people in their various institutions, from the home to the highest levels of church and government. Living close to the poor of the city, he had thought intensely about the responsibilities of man to his neighbors. When he became a master in the university, he lectured on these as well as on purely theological subjects.

For twenty or more years Stephen lived, studied, taught, and preached in the university community of Paris. Throughout these years he heard the tap-tap of the hammers of stonemasons at work on the cathedral of Notre Dame. The first stone of the great church had been laid about the time he was born. When he left Paris in 1206, the building had not been completed. Whenever Stephen walked in the streets, he saw scenes of life at all levels—highest to lowest. From these scenes he drew examples for his teaching and, in later years, for his sermons.

In Paris Stephen found that one of his country's martyr heroes, St. Thomas à Becket, champion of justice for all, was as much revered by the French as by the English. Thomas à Becket was the first archbishop of Canterbury to try to maintain the liberties of the church against the power of the king. The story of the quarrel between Becket and King Henry II was well known to the French. So, of course, was the account of Becket's murder in Canterbury cathedral by four of Henry's knights, who had been prompted by one of the king's intemperate remarks to do away with the archbishop.

The life of Becket had special significance to Stephen, whose childhood had coincided with the archbishop's last years. From his parents and their friends Stephen had heard with horror the story of the murder. He had been told about the king's anguish on hearing of the archbishop's death. Also, he had been told that Thomas, in one of his attempts to escape the king's wrath, had temporarily taken refuge in one of the Lincolnshire monasteries near the Langton manor.

Stephen's early adoption of some of the ideals of Thomas à Becket was not surprising. Many years after his student days Stephen was to be the first archbishop of Canterbury after Thomas to try to maintain the rights and liberties of the church against the king's power.

Stephen Langton believed in a fundamental law of right and wrong—a law that had its foundation in the Scriptures. He referred to the law sometimes as scriptural law and sometimes as the law of nature. This law, he maintained, was binding upon the pope, the king, and other high officials of church and state, as well as upon lesser men. Langton's conscience and his belief in the law were destined to cause him serious trouble in the future.

Usually Langton had no difficulty in accepting the authority of the pope or the king. A grievous problem arose when he received an order that conflicted with his conscience—that violated the fundamental law in which he believed. Such an order he refused to obey, and he accepted his punishment without complaint. Action of this kind, he believed, made him a true successor of St. Thomas à Becket. The disobedience that Stephen Langton and Thomas à Becket practiced was, in spirit, similar to the civil disobedience practiced more than six centuries later by Henry David Thoreau, Mahatma Gandhi, and Martin Luther King, Jr.

In his twenty or more years in Paris Stephen Langton was

not only an outstanding teacher and lecturer. As a doctor in the liberal arts and in theology he was a student of the Bible. He rearranged the chapters of the Bible to give them greater continuity. His rearrangement, with some modifications, is used today by both Catholics and Protestants.

He wrote comments on the Bible—comments that contained some observations upon social and political problems. To him life seemed to be a unit; it could not be rigidly compartmentalized.

He wrote poetry, some of it set to music as hymns. He wrote a rhymed psalter—a collection of the Psalms put to rhyme.

He was an eloquent preacher, in Latin, English, and French. Some of his sermons appeared under the name of Stephen with the Tongue of Thunder. He preached to the common people, as well as to students and to fellow churchmen.

Early in 1206 Pope Innocent III named Stephen Langton cardinal priest of St. Chrysogonus in Rome. When Langton left for his new position, he was probably the outstanding figure in the university community of Paris.

THE ELECTION

The year before Langton was called to Rome, Hubert Walter, forty-third archbishop of Canterbury, died in England, which was then ruled by King John, sometimes known as John Lackland. For more than six hundred years the archbishop of Canterbury had been the most powerful church official in all of England. He was the head of the church and a close adviser to the king. One of his traditional duties was to counsel the king on matters of both religion and state. One of the traditional obligations of the king was to seek counsel from the archbishop on matters of both state and religion.

Supposedly, each new archbishop was elected by the monks of the powerful Canterbury priory, Christ Church. His election had then to be confirmed by the pope in Rome. Actually, the archbishop usually was elected with the unwanted help or coercion of the king. Often the king's choice was a man more experienced in politics than in religion.

John's father, Henry II, had "helped" in the election of a church official by sending the following message to the supposed electors: "Henry king of the English to his faithful monks of the church of Winchester, greeting. We order you to hold a free election, but nevertheless forbid you to elect anyone except Richard my clerk, the archdeacon of Poitiers."

When Hubert Walter, who had been the archbishop for twelve years, died in July 1205, King John hurried from Buckinghamshire over to Canterbury. He wanted to help the monks of the priory choose Walter's successor. His candidate was his secretary, John de Gray, bishop of Norwich, more a politician than a churchman.

The Canterbury monks did not like King John's choice. Archbishop Walter and his predecessor had been political in their thinking and acting. The monks wanted a religious man for their archbishop. They wanted one of their own. They resisted John's attempts to coerce them.

Bishops of the province entered the scene. They claimed that they, too, had a right to share in the election. The monks disputed their claim. Growing impatient over the delay caused by the dispute, John announced that the election would be postponed until the end of November. Then he left Canterbury for another part of his kingdom.

A few weeks later the Canterbury monks heard a rumor that agents of King John were in Rome advancing the cause of John de Gray. They quickly held a secret election, chose their subprior, Reginald, and sent him off to Rome with a delegation of fellow monks. The monks hoped to see Pope Innocent III and persuade him to confirm Reginald as the new archbishop of Canterbury.

When John, through his agents in Rome, heard of these events, he went into one of those tempestuous rages for which his family was famous. He hurried again to Canterbury. There he faced the monks who had not gone to Rome. Cowed by the presence of John and his temper, the monks timidly and falsely assured the king that no election had been held.

John then took full charge of the situation. He told the monks and the bishops to end their dispute and hold an election at once. With the king looking on, the monks went through the motions of election and unanimously chose John de Gray. At John's command, the bishops, who were not allowed to vote, gave their approval of de Gray. Only the approval of the pope was required before de Gray would become the forty-fourth archbishop of Canterbury.

Early in 1206 a second delegation of Canterbury monks, this one to announce the election of John de Gray, arrived in Rome and appeared before Pope Innocent III.

The pope was at first understandably puzzled by the conflicting claims of the two delegations. Reginald and his fellow monks claimed that the second election was invalid. Monks of the second delegation claimed that Reginald had not been duly elected; he had not received the approval of the bishops of the province.

After listening to the arguments of each delegation, the pope quashed the elections of both Reginald and John de Gray; he said the elections had been irregular. In December 1206 he called for another election, this one by the Canterbury monks then in Rome. The vote was a tie; half of the monks voted for

Reginald, half of them for de Gray. The pope then asked the monks to consider a new candidate, Stephen Langton, an Englishman in his late forties who had been born in Lincolnshire. He told them that Langton, cardinal priest of St. Chrysogonus in Rome, had for many years been a distinguished teacher and scholar at the University of Paris.

According to Roger of Wendover, one of the English chroniclers of the period, some of the monks objected to the pope's choice. Langton did not have King John's approval, which they thought was necessary. The pope assured them that such approval was not required. Then, under threat of excommunication, he ordered the monks "to elect as archbishop the man whom we give you as a father and as pastor of your souls."

Dreading excommunication—complete separation from the church—which they believed would damn their souls to hell, the monks consented to the pope's choice. They elected Stephen Langton the forty-fourth archbishop of Canterbury.

The pope was pleased. He recalled that when he was in Paris as Lotario di Segni, many years before he became Pope Innocent III, he and Langton had been fellow students. The monks were pleased that the pope was pleased. The pope sent King John a letter telling him of the election. He hoped for John's approval.

The king, when he learned of the election, was furious. He could not prevent Langton from being elected and consecrated as archbishop. But he could keep him from being installed at Canterbury—or from living in England. And for six years he did.

THE INTERDICT

King John's first letter to the pope after the monarch knew of Langton's election as archbishop of Canterbury bristled with fury and indignation. The king declared that Langton was unknown in England; worse, that he had lived for many years among enemies in a foreign land; still worse, that he had been elected to a high English office without the consent of an English king.

The pope replied that John had written "insolently and impudently as though threatening and expostulating." The king had offered only "paltry reasons" for not granting his consent to the election.

"We are surprised," wrote the pope, "that a man of so great a name, a native of your own kingdom, could have remained unknown to you at least in reputation, especially since after his promotion to the cardinalate you wrote to him that, though you had planned to summon him to the service of your household, you rejoiced at his elevation to a greater office."

Messengers and a letter had been sent from Rome to ask John's assent to Langton's election, but no reply had been received, the pope wrote.

"Wherefore, we do not think it necessary to ask again for the king's consent after all these approaches; but, swerving neither to the right nor to the left, we have resolved to follow the course appointed by the canonical decrees of the holy fathers—namely, that no delay or difficulty should be allowed to thwart good arrangements, lest the Lord's flock should for a long time be without pastoral care."

On receiving the pope's letter, John was again furious. He showed little concern for the Lord's flock or its pastoral care. Instead, he ordered the Canterbury monks expelled from their monastery and their revenues confiscated. He sent two of his knights with armed attendants hurrying to Canterbury to carry out his orders. With swords drawn the two knights and their men burst into the monastery. In the king's name they ordered that all the monks should leave England at once. If the monks delayed, their monastery and they in it would be set afire. Without delay the monks left, and many of them spent several years as refugees in French monasteries.

Pope Innocent responded at first to John's violence by waiting and by hoping the king would approve of Langton's election. When he had waited a few months, he decided to consecrate Langton as archbishop of Canterbury without John's approval. The consecration took place on June 17, 1207, nearly two years after the death of Archbishop Walter. It took place not in Canterbury, England, but in Viterbo, Italy.

In August the pope wrote to three English bishops he thought he could trust—the bishops of London, Ely, and Worcester. He instructed them to try to persuade John to "bow to the divine ordinance," the election of Langton. If they failed, they were to proclaim an interdict throughout England. In a later letter he added Wales. To many people of the thirteenth century living under an interdict by a pope was a horrendous experience. It meant their almost complete separation from the church while they were living and exposure to hell's fires after death.

In November the pope followed his letters to the three bishops with an open letter to the English nobles. He urged them to save the king "from rejecting the counsel of good men and from walking in the counsel of the ungodly"—that is, he urged the nobles to urge the king to accept Stephen Langton as archbishop of Canterbury.

The pope's letter, dated November 21, began with this warning:

To all the noble magnates of England.

If to our well-beloved son in Christ, John, illustrious king of the English, you pay the loyalty that is his due, be assured that this is pleasing both to God and to us. But because you should regulate your loyal attachment to the earthly king so as never to offend the

Heavenly King, being upright and loyal men you ought to be on guard to save the king by your fathful advice from a policy which he has seemingly planned in enmity to God—that of persecuting our venerable brother Stephen, archbishop of Canterbury, and, through him, the church committed to his charge.

At about the same time Stephen Langton addressed a letter to the English people. He wrote as an Englishman who had always been faithful to his king. Since his earliest days, he wrote, he had been devoted to England and had felt changes in his country's fortunes as if they were his own. He had also been devoted to the cause of church independence, for which Thomas à Becket had died. This independence was now in danger, and all Englishmen should come together to rescue it. Those unable to meet the king face to face should use persuasion with friends and neighbors.

"By human law," he wrote, "a slave is not bound to serve his lord in vile deeds, much less you who are free. . . . Hence, whatever service is rendered to the temporal king to the prejudice of the eternal king is undoubtedly an act of treachery."

To men of the knightly class, he pointed out that, as they had received their insignia from the church, they had a duty to the church.

King John did not "bow to the divine ordinance," and the interdict on England and Wales was proclaimed in the spring of 1208. It permitted no traditional church services but the baptism of infants and the confession of the dying. People were not to be married by the clergy in churches—that is, they were not to be married. Nor were they to be buried in ground consecrated by the church. They were to be denied the sacraments of the altar, such as holy communion. Sermons, if any, were not to be preached in churches.

John reacted to the interdict by confiscating church property. He became more tyrannical.

The pope threatened sterner measures. In November 1209 Langton, with the approval of the pope, excommunicated John. The king was now an outlaw from the church. If he should die, his soul would be in danger of hell's fire—or so the pope, most of the people of England, and John himself believed. The king's power over his subjects was lessened. If they chose not to follow a king outlawed by the church, their consciences would not torment them.

High church officials left England. By the end of 1211 only one bishop remained. Many of the nobles, who saw their own rights and privileges threatened by John's arbitrary acts, talked secretly of resistance—even rebellion. The common people fretted under the interdict. Even though the interdict was not everywhere strictly enforced, it disrupted their normal lives. For more than five years, from the spring of 1208 to the summer of 1213, people could not be properly married or buried.

Archbishop Langton made several attempts to meet with John. At least twice he landed at an English port, but John refused him the safe conduct that would have saved him from being hanged if he had gone inland. Much of the six years between March 1207 and May 1213 Langton spent quietly at Pontigny, the great Cistercian monastery in France where Thomas à Becket had previously found refuge.

KING JOHN'S SURRENDER

Suddenly and unexpectedly, more than five years after the interdict had been imposed, King John ended his quarrel with the pope. A Welsh chieftain and his followers had revolted. As John prepared to go to Wales to quell the revolt, he heard a rumor that some of his English nobles were conspiring to drive him from the kingdom and choose someone else as king. He heard another rumor, that he was to be murdered in battle if he went to war against the Welsh. Two leaders of the conspiracy, Robert fitz Walter and Eustace de Vesci, fled the country. John had their castles destroyed as he looked about for more conspirators.

At this critical time William Marshal, the earl of Pembroke, a trusted follower, advised the king to make peace with the pope. John accepted the advice. But he went further in his concessions than anyone had expected. In a charter of May 15, 1213, John, king of England and lord of Ireland, offered and freely yielded "to God, and His holy apostles Peter and Paul, and to the Holy Roman Church our mother, and to the lord pope Innocent and his catholic successors, the whole kingdom of England and the whole kingdom of Ireland, with all their rights and appurtenances, for the remission of our sins and the sins of our whole family, both living and dead; so that from henceforth we hold them from him and the Roman Church as a vassal."

Although John was still king of England and lord of Ireland, he had made England and Ireland a feudal fief of the church of Rome and himself subject to orders of the pope. He would have to accept Stephen Langton as archbishop of Canterbury.

About two months later Archbishop Langton landed in England. On St. Margaret's Day, July 20, 1213, the archbishop with several bishops and other clergy met the king with his nobles and knights in front of Winchester cathedral. In a splendid and solemn ceremony, the king swore on a Bible that he would love and defend the church, reinstate the good laws of his predecessors, especially the laws of the revered King Edward the Confessor, annul bad laws, judge all men according to the just proceedings of his court, and give to every man his historic rights.

Then in an emotional scene at the door of the cathedral church, the archbishop formally absolved John from excommunication. The ceremony ended with the chanting of the fifty-first psalm, which contained the lines:

Averte faciem tuam peccatis meis, et omnes iniquitates meas dele,
Cor mundum crea in me, Deus.

In the King James version of the Bible these are translated as:

Hide thy face from my sins, and blot out all mine iniquities.
Create in me a clean heart, O God.

The archbishop, the king, and their followers then entered the church, where mass was celebrated. Afterward, according to Roger of Wendover, "The archbishop, bishops, and nobles feasted at the same table with the king, amidst joy and festivity."

Despite the "joy and festivity," neither the archbishop nor the dissident nobles approved of the terms on which King John had made peace with the pope. Most of the dissidents regarded John's action as a disgraceful surrender of the kingdom. Langton, a man of principle and an Englishman to his innermost heart, regarded the act as a betrayal of the people—as a great and unnecessary blunder.

As archbishop of Canterbury and adviser to the king, Langton now had three important aims: to restore to the churches the properties John had taken from them, to assure that good men were appointed or elected to church offices, and to promote sound and just government.

In no more than a month after Langton's arrival in England an order was issued in the king's name that the laws of King Henry I, John's great-grandfather, should be observed throughout the kingdom, that all unjust laws should be abolished, and that sheriffs and other agents of the king should refrain, "as they regarded life and limb," from such physical or other abuse of anyone, or such unlawful practices, as had been their custom.

Here was the quiet, unobtrusive Langton at work. Obviously, the archbishop believed that sound and just government could be promoted better by citing King Henry's published laws (which included his coronation charter, sometimes known as a charter of liberties) than by referring to the vague ideals associated with Edward the Confessor—ideals that existed principally in people's minds. Issued in 1100 to help secure a shaky claim to the throne, Henry's charter was addressed to the nobles of his time, but it mentioned other citizens and their rights. Langton was already laying the groundwork for a charter greater than Henry's.

AFTER WINCHESTER

Archbishop Langton was soon to remind King John of the oath so solemnly sworn at Winchester. Many nobles of the northern counties had refused to furnish men and money for a military expedition that John was planning for the recovery of ancestral land he had lost in France. They sent word that the king had no right to make demands upon them for such an overseas expedition; besides, they had already spent most of their money in his service.

A month after he had taken his oath at Winchester, John temporarily abandoned his overseas expedition, hastily collected an army, mostly mercenaries, and started north to punish the defiant and disobedient nobles.

When he heard of the king's action, the archbishop was instructing a council at St. Paul's Cathedral in London on the laws of Henry I. Leaving the council abruptly, he set out after

John and his army. At Northampton, about sixty miles from London, he caught up with them. He pleaded with the king not to break the promises so solemnly made at Winchester. Such matters as the action of the dissident northern nobles, Langton said, should be submitted to the king's court for judgment.

John refused to listen and pushed ahead with his army. Langton followed them to Nottingham, sixty miles farther. There the archbishop threatened to excommunicate anyone (except the king) who continued to take part in the punitive expedition. He did not turn back toward London until John had named a convenient date for the rebellious nobles to come to his court and seek justice. For a few more days the king and his army marched about the countryside, but they did little harm.

To Pope Innocent III England was a vassal state. John had surrendered his kingdom to the church at Rome. He had renewed his pledge of fealty and obedience in the absolution ceremony at Winchester. At about the time John renewed his pledge, Innocent addressed a letter to the English king, nobles, and clergy. He informed them that he was sending to their island his legate Nicholas, bishop of Tusculum, an emissary with supreme powers—powers superior to those of even the archbishop of Canterbury. Nicholas would serve as "an angel of salvation and peace."

In the opinion of Archbishop Langton, Nicholas was not an angel of any kind. He interfered in church appointments and elections. He was lenient with King John about the restoration of confiscated church properties. He made few contributions to sound and just government. When Nicholas returned to Rome a year later, he gave the pope an unfavorable report on the archbishop. Langton was thinking and acting more like an Englishman than an agent of the pope.

Peace between the king and the pope had not brought

peace or security to the people of England. It had not given them the rights and liberties the king had sworn at Winchester that he would restore to them. John had failed to keep his word. Both nobles and common people were restless. But, with the new archbishop of Canterbury at last among them, they were hopeful. Many of the dissident nobles joined the archbishop in seizing on the charter of Henry I as a wedge they could use for prodding John into restoring the historic rights of Englishmen.

Henry had promised in his coronation charter that the church should be free from interference by the king, that if anyone should be convicted of treason or other crime, his punishment should be "according to his fault" ("Let the punishment fit the crime"), that the laws of King Edward should be restored, and that certain evil practices should be stopped.

One of the evil practices Henry mentioned in the charter related to the taxes on inheritance of property rights. Henry promised that, on the death of any baron or other person holding property rights from the king, the heir should not pay an oppressive inheritance tax, as in the recent past, but only "a just and lawful relief." To this promise the king added a provision favorable to the common people: "And in like manner, too, the dependants of my barons shall pay a like relief for their land to their lords."

Another evil practice mentioned in the charter was the taking of property in exchange for the king's permission for a woman to marry. Henry promised in the charter that "if any baron or other subject of mine shall wish to give his daughter, his sister, his niece, or other female relative, in marriage, let him ask my permission on the matter; but I will not take any of his property for granting my permission, nor will I forbid his giving her in marriage except he wishes to give her to an enemy of mine; . . . and I enjoin on my barons to act in the same way towards the sons and daughters and wives of their dependants."

In directing that the rights he was granting to the barons should be given by the barons to their "dependants," Henry was approaching the concept of equal rights for men of all classes.

GATHERING OF THE BARONS

In November 1214 many of King John's barons and other nobles journeyed to Bury St. Edmunds in Suffolk as if they were on a religious pilgrimage. However, their real purpose was not religious. It was to plot secretly about how to regain from John the liberties they believed should be theirs—such liberties as had been included by Henry I in his coronation charter.

"And so they all gathered in St. Edmund's church," wrote Roger of Wendover, "and starting with the most eminent they all swore on the high altar that, if the king refused to grant them the said liberties, they would go to war against him, and withdraw their allegiance, until he should confirm by a charter under his own seal everything they should require."

Early in January 1215 a group of nobles, all of them armed, appeared at a council King John was holding in London. Most of them stood watching tensely as their leaders advanced and spoke with the king.

The leaders reminded King John that they and other English people had been granted certain rights by kings who had ruled before him. They reminded him that in his coronation oath he had promised to continue those rights. They then demanded that the king restore to them the ancient rights and liberties which, they said, the king had taken from them.

[*31*]

King John was furious. He tried to make the leaders withdraw their demands and promise not to renew them. This they refused to do.

Reluctantly the king agreed to meet the rebellious nobles at Northampton on April 26, Low Sunday, the Sunday after Easter. He promised that there and then he would give an answer to their demands.

King John spent much of the next four months preparing for war. He brought hired or mercenary troops over from mainland Europe. He had his already well-fortified castles stocked with food and ammunition. He ordered the construction of siege weapons that could be used to batter down the castles of his rebellious subjects.

The rebel nobles, too, prepared for war. They hurried to fortify their castles and to train or retrain the knights and other men of their own small armies. They tried to win other nobles over to their cause.

Who were those rebels of 1215? Most of them lived in northern and eastern counties of England, but they had sympathizers throughout the kingdom. Many of them were young. In some families, the father remained loyal to King John even though one or more of his sons rode off to join the rebels, who became commonly known as the barons.

During the week after Easter well-armed barons of the northern counties gathered with their forces at Stamford and began marching southward. As they marched, they were joined by other rebels. By the time they reached Northampton they had been joined by rebels from eastern and southern counties.

The rebel force arrived at the appointed place at the appointed time. But the king was not there. He was at his hunting lodge near Salisbury, many miles to the south.

For several weeks Archbishop Langton had been working

hard for a peaceful settlement of the quarrel between the king and his rebellious subjects. During the second week after Easter, with William Marshal, the earl of Pembroke, and other representatives of the king, Langton met the barons near Brackley, about twenty miles southwest of Northampton. At Brackley he received written demands that the king restore the good old laws and legal customs of the realm. These demands included a return to the laws of Edward the Confessor and to the promises in the coronation charter of Henry I. If the king did not peacefully grant their demands, the dissidents declared, they would use force.

Langton believed that the demands of the baronial force were just, and he advised the king to accept them. But he strongly disapproved of the threat of force.

Through the archbishop and other advisers, the king made counterproposals. The rebels rejected them. On May 3 they defied the king. They formally renounced their homage and fealty. This act was their declaration of independence.

In battle formation the rebels left Brackley, marched back to Northampton, and laid siege to one of the king's castles. Unlike the king, they had no siege weapons. So for more than a week they stood and sat and slept before the king's Northampton castle without being able to take it. Then they moved on to capture a less important castle where they had a sympathizer.

As leader of the army they had assembled, the barons chose Robert fitz Walter, lord of Dunmow, a powerful earl from eastern England, who had conspired against John after a Welsh chieftain had revolted. They gave him the imposing title Marshal of the Army of God and Holy Church. But the title gave them little success in capturing King John's castles.

For a while the two sides, the king's and the barons', were

almost equally balanced. Each side competed for the allegiance of the undecided or weakly committed nobles. Each side wanted to end the quarrel through negotiations.

Then, early on a Sunday, May 17, the rebel forces captured London, "the capital of the crown and realm." They were let into the city by friends, and they took possession with little resistance from the Londoners. Possibly many of the London citizens thought they might fare better under the barons than under the king.

Except for small skirmishes, fighting stopped. The rebel Army of God and Holy Church stayed in or near London. The king, in his castle at Windsor, kept his troops from attacking.

Into this lull in the civil war stepped the moderates of each side—men less violently sure than most that their side was right and the other side wrong. They were guided by Archbishop Langton, more than usual the quiet, unobtrusive figure. Sometimes he was with the king, sometimes with the rebels. What did he say to them? Who knows what a medieval archbishop says to a king or to a group of rebellious nobles—or what they say to him?

Under letters of safe conduct the archbishop and the moderates rode forth and back, forth and back between the rebels in London and King John in his castle at Windsor. They hoped to hammer out terms that both parties would accept.

Which events happened on which days of June 1215 are matters for speculation. Historians specializing in research on Magna Carta have speculated for more than two centuries without coming to total agreement. For their information they have had to depend mostly on a few letters of safe conduct, royal writs, and similar papers that survived the hectic days of a civil war.

Most recent historians have doubts about the June 15 date for Magna Carta. They do not believe that June 15 was the date on which the king's great seal was affixed to the document. They have stated that Magna Carta as we know it today was not even written until after June 15.

TWO DOCUMENTS BEFORE MAGNA CARTA

A short time before Magna Carta and closely related to it were two other important documents. One of these, the Articles of the Barons, was written only a few days or weeks before Magna Carta. It was loaded with specific demands for the rights dearest to the barons, men of property and privilege.

The other document is called by historians the Unknown Charter of Liberties. This document with the curious name was not really a charter; it had no royal signature or seal. Neither was it really unknown. It had rested for centuries in the French royal archives, but it was little noticed by English historians until in 1893 one of them called special attention to it. It had been written possibly in November 1213 or a short time later, probably in the hope that King John would read and accept it. For its ideas it drew heavily from the coronation charter of Henry I.

More idealistic than the Articles of the Barons, the Unknown Charter of Liberties begins, "King John concedes that he will not take men without judgment, nor accept anything for doing justice, nor perform injustice." By "judgment" was meant the decision of a court of law. This first item was intended to keep the king from imposing sentence as if he were judge and jury and also from accepting bribes for doing justice.

The charter ends, "And I [King John] concede that no man shall lose life or limb for Forest offences." In the reigns of John and his father, Henry II, penalties for the taking of deer and the cutting of wood in the king's forest had been very severe and included death.

Between the two sentences quoted above are ten other

items relating to rights and privileges demanded for the nobles, their families, and the common people.

In the writing of the Unknown Charter of Liberties Stephen Langton was again the quiet, unobtrusive figure. If where he was and when are considered, he could easily have been one of the anonymous authors—perhaps the principal author. He had been deeply disturbed by the discontent of both the nobility and the common people. The most idealistic items in the charter were characteristic of his speaking and writing; they embodied his ideals for bringing about peace through law and justice.

For about a year after his return to England Langton had been in almost constant communication with the barons. He had great influence among them. They knew he was in sympathy with their demands for the restoration of the old rights and liberties included by Henry I in his coronation charter. After several months they knew also that he appeared unable to convince King John to restore those rights.

Without doubt, both the Articles of the Barons and the Unknown Charter of Liberties formed the basis for Magna Carta. Written into all three documents were insistent demands for a renewal of the old rights.

Only one copy of the Articles of the Barons was made, historians believe. Like one of the copies of Magna Carta, it is now under glass in the British Museum. It is a vellum sheet, longer and narrower than the great charter—21¾ inches long and 10½ inches wide.

At the head of the sheet are these Latin words: "*Ista sunt Capitula que Barones petunt et dominus Rex concedit.*" In English: "These are the articles [*capitula*] that the Barons request and the lord King grants."

The document contains forty-nine *capitula,* all in Latin and

[*36*]

all, like the title, in hand lettering similar to that used by the king's clerks. At the bottom of the sheet is the king's great seal and a small piece of faded purple ribbon.

RUNNYMEDE

On June 8, 1215, letters of safe conduct were issued by King John's forces for the period from June 9 to midnight of June 11 to agents of the barons who were coming to the king "to make and secure peace." According to an old record King John and Archbishop Langton were "at the meadow of Staines," Runnymede, on June 10. Probably there and then John was presented with the Articles of the Barons and was forced to accept certain of them as a basis for later agreement.

The truce of June 9–11 was extended to June 15, and the stage was set for the large and historic meeting of the two forces at Runnymede.

A traditional assembly ground, Runnymede was between the London headquarters of the rebel barons and the Windsor headquarters of the king. When the rebel force and the royalist force met there on June 15, each side was suspicious of the other. Neither trusted the other.

The rebels had chosen nearby Staines as their base. There they had gathered their men, their weapons, their horses, and pitched their tents and pavilions. Staines lay on the north bank of the River Thames. Windsor lay on the south bank. The direct route between the two forces was over Staines bridge, where the old Roman road from London crossed the river.

Almost an island, Runnymede was protected in part by marshy ground. The barons could be sure that, when they entered this area from the east, the king's forces could approach only down the southern bank of the river. Negotiations would be carried out in the open or under canvas pavilions.

[*37*]

For several days the usually quiet water-meadows of Runnymede resounded with the clank of armor, the thud of horses' hoofs, the sharp commands of officers. Both the barons' and the king's men had come to the conference fully armed.

On June 15 and perhaps on the following days, too, the king and the barons met, argued, and negotiated. With the help of Stephen Langton, they finally arrived at terms both sides would accept.

Perhaps June 15 is inscribed on Magna Carta (which was not called that until about ten years later) because on that date the king and the barons agreed, or agreed to agree, on final peace terms. After the terms had been agreed to, they had to be expressed in Latin words and sentences that meant the same to both sides. The words and sentences, arranged in sixty-three articles or *capitula,* had to be inscribed with a goose-quill pen on a vellum sheet.

Probably by June 19 a rough draft of the charter had been completed. On that day came what has been called a "firm" peace. The barons renewed their homage to King John. The king sent out orders to his agents and soldiers throughout the realm to refrain from further acts of war. On June 23 tents were struck, and the meeting at Runnymede moved into history.

On June 19 the king had ordered that the charter should be read in public throughout the realm. By June 24 copies of the charter, with the king's great seal attached, had gone to at least twenty-one counties.

A recently discovered manuscript provides unexpected information about the distribution of Magna Carta. This manuscript—apparently there were others like it—is a translation of Magna Carta into thirteenth-century French vernacular, which was then the common language of the ruling class in

England as well as France. It is addressed to the sheriff and elected knights of each shire of England and instructs them to seize the land and chattels of all who refuse to take an oath to obey the twenty-five barons named in the charter; the recently found copy is addressed in particular to the sheriff and elected knights of Hampshire. Evidently, someone thought Magna Carta was sufficiently important to deserve special treatment—to be distributed not only in the official Latin but in a language the nobles and King John could more readily understand.

MAGNA CARTA, 1215

Magna Carta has been called the result of selfish action by a few powerful men—certain barons, earls, and nobles of other rank in the English peerage. In medieval England each of the nobles (while in power) owned and lived in one or more well-fortified castles. The military value of a castle was then very high. Whoever ruled the castles ruled the realm. John and other English kings of the medieval period believed that castles not held by the crown should be held by men loyal to the king, men always ready and willing to come to the aid of the king with other men armed with swords, crossbows, and battle-axes. Punishment for a nobleman's disloyalty commonly included demolition of his castle or, more often, confiscation by the crown.

Between 1154 and 1214 the ratio of baronial to royal castles was greatly reduced, a student of medieval England has reported. In 1154 the 225 baronial castles outnumbered the 49 royal castles by a ratio of almost 5 to 1. By the end of 1214, the year before Magna Carta, the number of baronial castles was 179, royal castles 93; the crown held more than one third of the castles.

The nobles of Stephen Langton's times were probably not aware of these statistics. But most of them must have been uncomfortably aware that some of their fellow nobles were losing their lives as well as their castles. Some of them were probably wondering whose castle would be the next to be demolished or confiscated.

Certainly self-interest, the protection of baronial property and the legal rights of the nobility, is evident in most of Magna Carta. Some of the chapters, such as those related to inheritances and marriages, apply only to the nobility. But the charter includes more than the rights of men of noble rank. Some chapters deal with fundamental human rights. In these chapters are the Latin equivalents for "free man," "man," "anyone." Although in 1215 the meaning of "free man" (*liber homo*) varied, usually the term referred to someone in the feudal scale next below the nobility. The terms "man" and "anyone" included the serf and others low in the scale, as well as the noble and the free man.

Probably Stephen Langton was responsible for these inclusive terms in the charter. If not he, then who? He had a lofty concept of what a kingship should be and a belief in right and justice for all men. At all stages of the negotiations that produced the charter he had positions of influence. Pieces of historical evidence, including letters of safe conduct, point to his importance: chief mediator between the king and the barons from the autumn of 1213 till the end of negotiations, participant in all the preliminary discussions between the king and the barons, arbitrator at Runnymede.

Perhaps because the archbishop had a hand in the writing of Magna Carta, the first chapter deals with freedom of religion. In it King John promised that the English church would be free from government interference and would "have its rights undiminished and its liberties unimpaired."

Most of the barons lived in isolated castles scattered throughout the country. But the great charter that they, with the help of Stephen Langton, wrung from King John included certain rights of the people living in cities and villages. In chapter thirteen the king promised to the city of London "all its ancient liberties and free customs, both by land and by water." To all other cities, boroughs, towns, and ports he promised "all their liberties and free customs."

In chapter twenty-eight he promised relief to humble tillers of the soil who had experienced the distress of having their grain or other produce taken from them without payment. This chapter provided that no constable or any other of the king's bailiffs "shall take any man's grain or other chattels unless he pays cash for them at once or can delay payment with the agreement of the seller."

Chapter thirty is similar to chapter twenty-eight: "No sheriff or bailiff of ours or anyone else is to take horses or carts of any free man for carting without his agreement."

Chapters thirty-eight, thirty-nine, and forty are the rugged and vigorous ancestors of the cherished concept of legal justice in the United States.

> 38. Henceforth no bailiff shall put anyone on trial by his unsupported allegation, without bringing credible witnesses to the charge.
> 39. No free man shall be taken or imprisoned or disseised [deprived of property] or outlawed or exiled or in any way ruined, nor will we go or send against him, except by the lawful judgment of his peers or by the law of the land.
> 40. To no one will we sell, to no one will we deny or delay, right or justice.

Archbishop Langton and the barons were aware that good laws do not guarantee justice unless the men appointed or elected to enforce them are well-informed and honest. In chapter forty-five John promised that "we will not make justices, constables, sheriffs, or bailiffs who do not know the law of the land and mean to observe it well."

Some of the persons involved in the writing of Magna Carta—certainly Stephen Langton—believed that men in high places who have been given certain rights should give those same rights to the men under them—a belief approaching the concept "that all Men are created equal." And so chapter sixty is addressed by King John to the barons and to officials of the church: "All the aforesaid customs and liberties which we have granted to be held in our realm, as far as it pertains to us toward our men, shall be observed by all men of our realm, both clergy and laymen, as far as it pertains to them, toward their own men."

Perhaps most unexpected of the chapters in Magna Carta is sixty-one, in which King John acknowledged the right of his subjects to punish him for violating terms of the charter he had sworn to uphold. Directly or indirectly the king acknowledged the right of revolution.

In this chapter John agreed that the barons should name any twenty-five of them who, "with all their might," would "observe, maintain, and cause to be observed the peace and liberties" granted in the charter. If John or his officials violated any of "the articles of peace or security" in the charter and did not "redress the offense within forty days" of the time the violation was brought to his attention, the twenty-five barons, "with the community of all the land," should "distrain and distress" the king in every way they could, "namely by seizing castles, lands, and possessions."

The king expected that his own life and the lives of his queen and children would be spared. Also, he expected that after the offense had been redressed, or amends had been made, his people would obey him as they had done before.

Of course, some details of this chapter, such as the taking of castles and the naming of twenty-five barons, have become obsolete. But the principle persists—the right of the people to punish a ruler for failing to carry out his sworn duties. The founding fathers of the United States wrote this principle into the Constitution in the paragraphs on impeachment.

The closing chapter of Magna Carta was a reminder of Archbishop Langton's experience with the pope. In it King John wished and firmly commanded "that the English Church shall be free, and the men in our realm shall have and hold all the aforesaid liberties, rights, and concessions well and peacefully, freely and quietly, fully and completely, for themselves and their heirs, from us and our heirs, in all things and places, forever."

AFTER MAGNA CARTA

Archbishop Langton saw in Magna Carta a code of law established at the insistence of the subjects of an imperious king. Merely by existing, it was a continuing condemnation of the arbitrary rule of one man. The archbishop must have hoped that with the passage of time it would become generally valued and respected. He could not have foreseen that in the future the spirit and the total meaning of the charter would be called up again and again, in England and elsewhere, as a defense against threats to the traditional liberties he valued. Nor could he have foreseen that the charter would be given new interpretations to fit new conditions.

Though the charter was formally sealed and accepted, it was soon violated by King John and extremist barons. Within two months of the peaceful settlement at Runnymede signs of hostilities were evident.

The pope's response to a report John had written in May, a short time before the Runnymede gathering, was a letter sharply critical of Archbishop Langton for not having taken strong action against the rebellious barons. It was addressed to the bishop of Winchester, the abbott of Reading, and Pandulf, the pope's legate in England, as members of a special commission. Of the rebel barons the pope wrote that "we excommunicate all such disturbers of the king and kingdom, together with their accomplices and supporters, and we lay their lands under interdict, most strictly requiring the archbishop and bishops to have these sentences solemnly published throughout England every Sunday and every feast day, with the tolling of bells and candles extinguished, until, having made amends to the king for the losses and wrongs inflicted on him, they humbly return to his service. If any bishop should avoid obeying our order, let him know that he is suspended from episcopal office."

When Langton was informed of the letter, he asserted that when it was received in August it was already out of date, that it had been written before the pope could have known of the settlement at Runnymede. Insisting that the sentences of excommunication and interdict were unjust, he refused to have a part in them.

"By human law, a slave is not bound to serve his lord in vile deeds, much less you who are free," he had written a few years before in a letter to the English people.

For his failure to cooperate in the excommunication and interdict he was suspended from office by the pope's commission. He received news of his suspension as he was setting out in late September for a council in Rome. He reacted to the suspension as a punishment to be accepted and borne without complaint, but he was saddened and depressed. The ideals of right and justice that he had stood for as a student, teacher, and man of the church seemed shattered. On his way to Rome he thought of becoming a hermit or of entering the Carthusian brotherhood, the most austere of the monastic orders.

Somewhere along the way, as he traveled southward, he must have passed close to an important letter being carried northward from Rome. The letter had been written by Pope Innocent after he had learned of Magna Carta. It began with the pope's interpretation of the situation in England: King John had been forced to accept at Runnymede an agreement that was shameful, base, illegal, and unjust. The letter ended with the pope's declaration that "we utterly reject and condemn this settlement, and under threat of excommunication we order that the king should not dare to observe it and the barons and their associates should not insist on its being observed. The charter, with all undertakings and guarantees, whether confirming it or resulting from it, we declare to be null and void of all validity for ever."

By the time the letter arrived in England the king and the rebel barons were again locked in bloody civil war.

In Rome Langton submitted without argument to the pope's confirmation of his suspension and then settled down for two and a half years of relatively quiet living.

In the fall of 1216, while on the offensive against rebel barons, King John contracted dysentery. In the early morning hours of October 18, while a furious wind howled about the battlements and nearby housetops, John died in the bishop of Lincoln's castle at Newark.

Pope Innocent III had died a few months before. Honorius III, who succeeded him, allowed Langton to return to England to resume his duties as archbishop of Canterbury. In the late winter or early spring of 1218 the archbishop made a leisurely journey homeward.

LAST YEARS

The England to which Archbishop Langton returned in 1218 was a country at peace with itself. Replacing John was the boy king Henry III, guided by a capable regent and counselors. The bitter feelings that had been part of the civil war were subsiding. They were being replaced by a general acceptance of the essential parts of Magna Carta.

For more than two years after his return to England Langton took only a minor part in affairs of the kingdom. Because of his opposition to the previous king and a previous pope, he was to some degree on probation. But 1220 was the year of the fiftieth anniversary of the martyrdom of St. Thomas à Becket. It was also the year of a second coronation of the boy king as Henry III.

A few weeks after this coronation the body of St. Thomas was removed from its tomb and, in a ceremony of pomp and magnificence, placed in a shrine in the cathedral at Canterbury. Archbishop Langton made the preparations and provided the hospitality for the occasion.

The ceremony had its symbolism. The crown and the church were at last giving St. Thomas the honor he deserved. In honoring him, the crown was recognizing one of Becket's ideals, that the church should be secure from unjustifiable interference by English kings.

Archbishop Langton was no longer on probation. When he went to Rome in October, he was warmly welcomed and asked to preach to the Italian people a sermon on the English saint Thomas à Becket.

As Archbishop Becket had claimed for the English church freedom from unjustifiable interference by English kings, so in Rome Langton claimed, and was assured of, freedom from unjustifiable interference by Italian popes.

On his way back to England Langton stopped in Paris for a nostalgic visit to the haunts he had known as a university student. When he reached England in August 1221, the pope's legate Pandulf was no longer there. Stephen Langton had no ecclesiastical superior in England. As archbishop of Canterbury, he was undisputed head of the church in England and chief adviser to the crown.

In 1225 Langton had an important part in arranging for a reissue of the great charter. Ten years before, the charter had been forced upon a reluctant king by rebellious subjects. Now it was widely accepted, even by men who had opposed it in 1215. It had become a symbol of unity and sound government. Langton had not changed. He was seeing his idea of kingship become reality: the king, like all other men, was subject to the law of the land.

The last eighteen months of Stephen Langton's life were unlike most of his adult years in England. From the Council of Oxford in January 1227 to his death in July 1228 the archbishop traveled little. He spent most of his time at Canterbury or at his manor house at Slindon, on the sunny slopes of the South Downs in Sussex.

Only once in the eighteen months did he travel to London to give the king his counsel. Three times the king journeyed to Canterbury to consult with him. At the age of about sixty-three Stephen had probably grown weary. Possibly he was ill.

Justice for all men and the liberties of his church were still important to him but less important than before. He was less a reformer. Now he was a peacemaker, a reconciler. He brought about reconciliation in an old quarrel between his brother Simon and the king. He made peace with the monks of Christ Church, Canterbury, who had opposed his plans for a rival collegiate church. Probably he was instrumental in keeping peace between the French and the English by persuading King

Henry not to undertake a war of conquest to recover his ancestral domains in France. He helped to bring peace in a
quarrel between Henry and the earl of Cornwall, Henry's
brother, who had a strong following of powerful barons.

In early July 1228 Stephen Langton performed what was
probably his last official act—as leader of a great memorial
celebration in honor of St. Thomas à Becket. The king and
members of his court were present. So were bishops and other
visiting clergy, as well as the monks of Canterbury. So were
large numbers of pilgrims. All were there to do homage to the
martyred archbishop, whose life had served as a model for
Langton's own.

Wearied by the strain of the king's visit and the great
celebration, Langton sought rest and relaxation at his Slindon
manor, possibly his favorite residence. There he died.

Historians can only guess at the year in which Stephen
Langton was born; they do not agree on the exact date of his
death or burial. They agree that he died at Slindon and was
buried at Canterbury. July 9, 1228, seems the most likely date
of his death and July 14 the most likely date of his burial.

These uncertainties are trivial. Important are the cer-
tainties: that Stephen Langton throughout most of his life
strove for justice and peace, that in his contributions to Magna
Carta he helped to establish, for all time, the concept of a
government of law based on fundamental human rights.

THREE

John Lilburne

A free press, religious liberty, voting rights for all free men, prison reform, the right of an accused person not to incriminate himself, an end to commercial monopolies—all of these ideals and more John Lilburne argued and fought and bled and suffered for in a time when they were new and strange to many of the people of England, and unacceptable to some of the most powerful.

As a boy growing up in northern England with a mind full of ideas of his own, John Lilburne was at one time "the greatest griefe" to his father. In the seventeenth-century London of King Charles I and Oliver Cromwell, Free-born John became the "griefe" to any man or group of men he believed threatened human liberty. The list is long. It includes bishops of the Church of England, the archbishop of Canterbury, the king, the House of Lords, the House of Commons, and the great Oliver Cromwell himself.

The loyalty of John Lilburne was not to persons or to institutions. It was to truths, principles, or ideals like those embodied in the American Declaration of Independence and the first ten amendments to the Constitution of the United States.

Lilburne paid dearly for his loyalties. He did not keep them to himself. Fearless and irrepressible, he shouted them out to the London crowds he easily gathered about him. A fluent, eloquent, and persuasive writer, he hastily scrawled down his ideas and had them printed in pamphlets that were eagerly snatched up and read by the people of London and other parts of England. Because his speaking and writing threatened the power of the powerful in church and state, he spent about half his adult life in the Tower of London or other prisons.

That John Lilburne should have become a champion of democratic ideals is one of those biographical paradoxes that add spice to history. For most of his early childhood he lived at Greenwich Palace near London. At this ancient royal palace on the River Thames, English kings and queens relaxed or held court. His parents were members of the courts of Queen Elizabeth and King James I.

John's father was Richard Lilburne, "the Sonne of a Gentleman." He was one of a large, ancient, and honorable family of County Durham in northern England. As a high-spirited, ambitious young man, Richard had come to London and the royal court in the service of "a very illustrious and noble earl," probably the earl of Northumberland. One of Richard's grandfathers, Bartholomew Lilburne, fully attired in armor, had attended King Henry VIII when that English king had met a French king, Francis I, in France on the Field of the Cloth of Gold at a gathering noted more for its splendor than for its useful results.

The Hixons, the family of John's mother, Margaret, were even more closely attached to the English royal court than the Lilburnes. Thomas Hixon, Margaret's father, had lived for many years at Greenwich Palace. He was Keeper or Gentleman of the Standing Wardrobe during the years Queen Elizabeth used to be rowed in the royal barge from Westminster down to Greenwich and back again. One of his duties was to see that the furniture and hangings of the palace were made ready for the arrival of the strong-willed Elizabeth and put in order after she left.

Appreciation of his services was expressed by an inscription over the east door of the Greenwich church attended by the Hixons: "Thomas Hixon of Greenwich, Esq., Soldier under Henry IV, K. of France, Gentleman of the Bedchamber to Q. Elizab. and Keeper of the Wardrobe."

No infant baptismal record for John Lilburne is known. Less solid evidence of when and where he was born indicates 1615 as the most likely date and Sunderland township, in County Durham, as the most likely place.

About ten years before John was born, his grandfather John Lilburne died and was buried in the family church near his home in the north country. As the eldest son, Richard inherited the family manor house and land in a township with the quaint name Thickley Punchardon. But Richard, Margaret, and their children continued for a time to live at Greenwich.

When John was about five years old, his mother died and was buried in the Greenwich parish church. His grandfather, Thomas Hixon, had died four months before.

[*51*]

Richard Lilburne now had better reasons for living at Thickley Punchardon than at Greenwich. Early in 1620, the year the *Mayflower* set sail for the New World, Richard and his four children, Elizabeth, Robert, John, and Henry, set sail for their new-old home in northern England. Down the Thames, into the North Sea, along the east coast of England they sailed, and then into the River Tyne to Newcastle, famous for its coal. There, after about two weeks aboard ship, they disembarked and traveled twenty-five miles overland by coach to the pleasant village of Auckland and about three more miles to the family manor at Thickley Punchardon. Lilburne's life can be divided into eight fairly distinct chapters. The journey to Thickley Punchardon was the beginning of the second chapter.

At Auckland stood St. Andrew's Church, where John's grandfather John and other Lilburnes lay buried. In the market place stood the grammar school, founded in 1604 by King James I for instructing boys in Latin, Greek, and English. There John and his brothers began their education, which they continued in a school at Newcastle. As sons of a country gentleman, they lived their early years close to the soil.

LONDON APPRENTICE

"After I came to have any discretion, well nigh twenty years agoe, my Father brought me to London," John recorded at a later time. And so began the third chapter of his life, far removed from the soil and not at the royal court. He was bound as apprentice to Thomas Hewson, a wholesale cloth merchant.

When John arrived in London, he was regarded by people he met as "rough-hewen" in speech and manners. He did not know how to doff his hat or to bow politely. But he was quick to learn and confident of his ability. "I had then as much mettle, life and spirit as most young men in London had," he wrote several years later.

In the shop of Thomas Hewson, who was a Puritan, John was given considerable responsibility. He worked hard and served his master faithfully. He handled money as well as bales of cloth. Evidently, he had some time for reading while he tended shop.

If John Lilburne was not a Puritan when he left home, he became one soon after his arrival in London. His reading included the Bible, John Foxe's *Book of Martyrs*, and the writings of Martin Luther, John Calvin, and other religious leaders. On Sunday mornings he rose early and, before sermon time, met with fellow apprentices to discuss the Scriptures.

The London to which Lilburne had come as an apprentice was a city of a quarter million inhabitants. It was pulsing with ideas, seething with questions—about religion, about politics, about human rights. The great William Shakespeare had died only a few years before, and people were still finding excitement in his plays presented in theaters along the riverbank. But more exciting to many than the plays of Shakespeare was the Bible.

For centuries the Bible, in Latin or Greek, was known to the English people only through their priests. It became known to them directly through the English translation known as the Great Bible of 1539. A copy of this Bible was ordered to be placed and chained in every church for all to see and to be read by those who could read. But a large book chained in a church is not readily accessible reading matter, and few other copies of the Bible were to be had.

Then, in 1611, about four years before John Lilburne was born, the Authorized King James Version was published. This version, beautiful in its language, made the Bible more widely available than before.

In the London known by young John Lilburne the people were not only reading the Bible. They were discussing it, interpreting it, arguing about it, writing pamphlets about it.

The Anglican Church, or Church of England, was the only one recognized by the government. But many persons had been influenced by the writings of Calvin and Luther. A number of dissident religious sects had sprung up. The largest were the Presbyterians and the Independents. They, the Congregationalists, and other smaller sects were often grouped under the name Puritan.

Able to read the Bible for themselves, members of these sects believed that they could find God without the aid of government-recognized priests and bishops. They believed they could make their own interpretations of the Scriptures. Further, many of them believed that one of their sacred liberties was the right to practice their religion as it was revealed to them through the Bible.

Queen Elizabeth had allowed an unusual degree of religious freedom. Under King James I, Anglican Church officials attempted to restrict activities of the dissident sects. Leaders of these sects responded to the attempted restrictions by greater activity, by sharp verbal attacks on the Anglican Church and its priests and bishops. Londoners went to see Shakespeare's plays during the week and on Sundays went to hear sermons as exciting to them as the plays. They were thrilled when they heard their Puritan pastors attack the Anglican bishops by such names as "traitors" and "anti-Christian mushrooms."

Puritan reaction to religious restrictions brought further restrictions. The further restrictions brought more violent reactions. England moved toward civil war.

YOUNG PURITAN

In 1636, when Lilburne was nearing the end of his apprenticeship, he was taken by his master to see Dr. John Bastwick, a Presbyterian with a ready pen and a dedication to the liberties that he and fellow Puritans believed were natural or God-given rights. Dr. Bastwick was spending time in the Gatehouse Prison for having written and printed pamphlets ridiculing the Anglican Church.

Being in prison had not kept the doctor from writing. Nor had it kept him from smuggling out what he wrote and having it secretly printed. He had recently written *The Letany*, one of his severest and most entertaining attacks against the Anglican Church. "From plague, pestilence, and famine, from bishops, priests, and deacons, good Lord deliver us" is a sample.

At that time the English government was trying to control printing through the Star Chamber, a court that acted as a licensing agency. Its aim was to prevent any criticism of church and government. The Star Chamber was widely dreaded and hated, but it was often defied. It could sentence men to prison without jury, witnesses, or other legal protections that accused persons now have. Most Englishmen believed that freedom of expression, which included the press, was a natural right they should not be denied. Hundreds of pamphlets were secretly printed and distributed in London and throughout the country without a license from the Star Chamber. Many writers and printers of these underground pamphlets were arrested and thrown into prison.

Lilburne was enthusiastic about the way Dr. Bastwick's *The Letany* cleverly and humorously ridiculed bishops of the Anglican Church. He believed it would help the Puritan cause if it could be printed and widely distributed. One day near the end of his apprenticeship, while visiting Dr. Bastwick in prison, he offered to take a manuscript copy of *The Letany* to Holland, have it printed there, and help smuggle thousands of copies into England.

Dr. Bastwick looked at the young man before him—slight of build, plainly dressed in the Puritan fashion, beardless, and with hair to his shoulders. At about twenty-one years of age, Lilburne seemed too young and inexperienced for a mission so dangerous for both of them. But his earnest eyes, his resolute mouth, and his almost fanatical enthusiasm finally won the doctor's approval of the mission. A few months later Lilburne was in Holland with a manuscript copy of *The Letany*. Here was the beginning of the fourth chapter of John Lilburne's life.

Before the middle of 1637 several thousand copies of *The Letany* were unloaded at English ports. Many of them were seized by government officials. A friend of Lilburne's who was supposed to receive the copies had turned informer.

The consequences were severe for Dr. Bastwick, two learned Puritan friends involved in the project, and eventually for Lilburne. In June the doctor and his two learned friends were tried before the Star Chamber and found guilty of seditious libel. They were sentenced to the pillory, to have their ears cut off, to be fined £5,000 each, and to be imprisoned for life.

In the New Palace Yard, thronged with people sympathetic to them and their cause, the three learned men courageously faced the pillory and the painful ordeal of having their ears cut off. Bastwick's wife kissed each ear and then his mouth.

With their necks clamped in the pillory and blood oozing from where their ears had been, the three men stood for hours and talked with the hundreds of people who pressed close about them to hear every word they spoke.

"Had I as many lives as I have hairs on my head, or drops of blood in my veins," Bastwick announced to the crowd, "I would give them all for this cause."

BEHIND THE CART

John Lilburne was still in Holland when Dr. Bastwick and his two friends lost their ears. He returned to London six months later with his zeal for the Puritan cause greater than when he left.

Warned by Dr. Bastwick's experience, he kept his sword constantly at his side as he went about London. While walking in a narrow lane on his way to see a Puritan friend, old John Wharton, he was set upon from behind and captured by government men before he could draw his sword. Taken to Gatehouse and later to the Fleet Prison, he was charged with importing "factious" and "scandalous" books from Holland.

After a hearing before the attorney general in mid-January 1638 Lilburne was brought to the Star Chamber office. A Bible was placed before him and he was told to remove his right glove and place his hand on the book.

"What to do, sir?" he asked.

"You must swear," was the answer.

"To what?"

"That you shall make true answer to all things that is asked you."

"Must I so, sir? But before I swear I will know to what I must swear."

"As soon as you have sworn, you shall."

"Sir, I am but a young man and do not well know what

belongs in the nature of an oath, and therefore before I swear I will be better advised."

Lilburne refused to take the oath. He said he doubted its lawfulness. He was told that other men had taken it. Did he claim to be wiser than other men? He replied that he cared not what other men had done. Although other Puritans had refused to take a similar oath before lower courts, Lilburne was the first man to refuse to take the Star Chamber oath.

On February 9, 1638, John Lilburne, about twenty-three years old, and John Wharton, about eighty-three years old, were called before the Star Chamber itself. They were accused of unlawfully printing Bastwick's *The Letany* and other libelous and seditious books. Neither the young man nor the old was awed by the stern lords of the Star Chamber glaring down at them. They were fortified by their religious faith. Later, in reporting the trial, Lilburne wrote that "the Lord according to his promise was pleased to be present with me by his speciall assistance, that I was inabled without any dantednesse of spirit, to speake unto that great and noble Assembly, as though they had beene but my equalls."

The lords of the Star Chamber were disturbed over Lilburne's attitude toward the court. Why had the prisoner refused to take the oath?

Lilburne replied that the oath was not according to the law of the land, which allowed no man to accuse himself. It was not according to the law of God, which allowed no man to destroy himself. It was not according to the law of nature, which expected every man to preserve himself. If a man was to be tried, before he took an oath he must be told what he was accused of and be permitted to face his accusers.

Lilburne said he was claiming the protection that the laws of the land and the Bible provided any free-born Englishman.

[*58*]

"Upon these grounds," he boldly told the court, "I did and do still refuse the oath."

When he was brusquely told to take off his glove and place his hand upon the Bible, he replied, "Most honorable and noble lords, . . . yet must I refuse the oath."

"This fellow," said a member of the Star Chamber, "hath been one of the notoriousest dispensers of libellous books that is in the kingdom, and"—he pointed to old John Wharton, who had likewise refused to take the oath—"that is the father of them all."

Three days later Lilburne and Wharton were again called before the Star Chamber. Again they refused to take the oath. The following day they were again brought before the court. To the charge of printing libelous and seditious books had been added the charge of "insufferable disobedience and contempt." Each of them was sentenced to be pilloried and to pay a fine of £500. Lilburne was given an additional sentence: to be tied to the tail of a cart and whipped through the streets of London from the Fleet Prison to New Palace Yard, two miles away.

News that the young man and the old had stood on their rights as free-born Englishmen and had refused to take the Star Chamber oath swept like a whirlwind through London. Many people were excited and elated. Young John Lilburne had suddenly won a high place in their affections. He had become "Free-born John," a popular hero.

In mid-April the sentences of Lilburne and Wharton were carried out. Like many other Puritans of their time, they called upon their religious faith to help them bear the punishment.

When Lilburne was led from the Fleet Prison, he said, "The will of my God be done." When he was stripped to the waist and his hands were tied to the back of the cart, he cried out, "Welcome be the cross of Christ!"

[*59*]

As the prisoner walked slowly behind the horse and cart through the London streets, every three or four steps his bare back was lashed with a corded whip having knots in it.

Friends and other sympathizers followed Lilburne along the two-mile route, shouting words of encouragement. One of them estimated that he suffered five hundred lashes.

As the blows fell, Lilburne recited lines of Scripture. Once he cried out, "Hallelujah, Hallelujah, Glory, Honor, and Praise be given to thee, O Lord, for ever."

With his neck in the pillory, the sun beating down on his head and bloody back, Lilburne addressed the sympathetic crowd that had gathered in New Palace Yard. He told the story of his arrest. He explained his reasons for refusing to take the Star Chamber oath. He attacked the Anglican bishops. He declared that the calling, power, and authority of the bishops were not from God or the king but from the devil. When he refused to stop talking, he was gagged so roughly that his mouth bled. At the end of two hours he was released from the pillory. Once his hands were free, he pulled from his pockets copies of three of Bastwick's pamphlets and tossed them to the crowd. As he was led back to the Fleet Prison large and enthusiastic crowds followed him. To them he was a hero. To the government he was a dangerous man.

At the Fleet Prison he was allowed to have a surgeon dress his bloody back. Then, feverish and exhausted, he was left without further care and with no food except that which friends and fellow prisoners smuggled in to him.

In a few days he was questioned by the warden of the Fleet Prison. Where had he got the copies of Bastwick's pamphlets he had tossed to the crowd at the pillory? When he refused to tell, he was removed to a dim inner part of the prison and kept there with iron chains on hands and legs. Only one person, an old woman, Katherine Hadley, was allowed to visit him.

Even under these terrible prison conditions Lilburne managed to write articles for pamphlets that were printed and widely circulated. Pen, ink, and paper had to be smuggled in to him, and his manuscripts smuggled out, probably by old Katherine Hadley or with the help of fellow prisoners.

His pamphlets were protests against the injustices of the government and the established church. They were demands for human rights and liberties. In one of them, *Come Out of Her My People*, he wrote, "I am resolved by the might and strength of my God, for the honour of my King and Country, and the good of future generations, to fight it out so long as I have a legge to stand on, and to waige professed warre so long as I have a drop of blood in my bellie: with the domestick and home bred enemies of the King and State for I have a Souldiers heart within my innocent breast."

Knowing that his activities might bring him to the pillory again—"or to a worse place"—he wrote that "by the strength and might of my God, I will, come life, come death, speak my mind freely and courageously."

On November 9, 1640, a petition for his release was presented to the House of Commons by Oliver Cromwell, a member for Cambridge. Clad in "a plain cloth-suit, which seemed to have been made by an ill country tailor," Cromwell spoke in a "voice sharp and untuneable" but with such "elequence full of fervour" that on November 13 Lilburne and other prisoners were liberated.

The following May, Commons pronounced the Star Chamber sentence against Lilburne illegal and characterized it as "Bloody, Wicked, Cruill, Barbarous, and Tyrannicall." It also granted him money as reparations.

[*61*]

The petition and the action of Commons set Lilburne free to continue his crusade for justice and free to go into business. He was free, also, to marry the courageous Elizabeth, daughter of Henry Dewell, a London merchant. She had been, he wrote in one of his pamphlets, "an object deare in my affections severall yeares before from me she knew anything of it." Before and after their marriage, she shared his ideals and worked loyally beside him. He said she was dearer to him than himself, "as she well deserved," and he treated her with a tenderness quite unlike the bravado with which he faced the rest of the world.

By the time Lilburne was released from the Fleet Prison he was determined to dedicate his life to a crusade against injustice and tyranny wherever he found them—a crusade for what he considered natural or God-given rights and liberties. As a result he was to spend much more time in prison. Because of his unswerving loyalty to his ideals, he was to lose several once-firm and valued friends. His father virtually disowned him, and of his several brothers only Henry stood by him in his later trials.

At the time of his first prison term his resolve "to waige professed warre" did not include violence. "I doe hold it unlawful," he wrote in *Come Out of Her My People*, "for any of God's people, in their greatest oppression by the Majestrate to rebel or to take up any Temporal armes against them."

He was soon to change his mind and to begin the fifth chapter of his life.

PURITAN SOLDIER

By early 1642 war between Parliament and King Charles I seemed certain. Lilburne had suffered under the government of the king. He believed that Parliament was sincere in its promise to "secure the Peoples' lawes and liberties." In the summer of 1642, when Robert Greville, Lord Brooke, was in London raising a regiment of foot soldiers for the Parliamentary army, Lilburne enlisted and was named a captain. When he went off to the war, Elizabeth went with him and for a time lived in quarters with him.

In late October Captain Lilburne fought in the indecisive battle of Edgehill. A greater test of his ability as a leader of men in war (as well as peace) happened about three weeks later near Brentford. A body of Royalist cavalry had burst out of the mist of a November morning, inflicted heavy losses on the Parliamentary regiment in front of Lord Brooke's, and started the men of both regiments retreating toward London.

Lilburne spurred his horse to a gallop, overtook the standard bearer of his regiment, and seized the colors. Shouting encouragement, he rallied the men, who faced about and fought gallantly against great odds. Lilburne himself was captured and taken to the king's headquarters at Oxford, where attempts were made to bribe him to join the Royalist forces.

When he refused to change sides, he was put in irons and kept a close prisoner in Oxford Castle. While a prisoner, he was several times marched to Oxford to appear before a Royalist judge to face charges of high treason, a crime punishable by death.

On December 13, through the wife of a fellow prisoner, he smuggled out a letter to Elizabeth. In this letter he enclosed another to the Speaker of the House of Commons. Both letters contained the information that on December 20 Lilburne and three other prisoners were scheduled to be tried for high treason; if tried, they would certainly be convicted and hanged.

The letter to the Speaker, promptly delivered by Elizabeth, was read in the House of Commons on Friday the six-teenth. On the following day the House published an announce-ment: if Parliamentary prisoners were hanged, Royalist pris-oners would be hanged in retaliation.

Although she was pregnant, Elizabeth set out in the wintry weather of late December with a letter from the Speaker to Judge Heath—a precious letter containing terms of the House of Commons announcement. She arrived at Royalist headquarters in Oxford just before the time set for the trial. Her "wisdome, patience, diligence," John Lilburne wrote later, saved his life.

Though his life was spared, Lilburne was kept in prison for several more months. He was freed in an exchange of prisoners the following spring. On his return to London, wrote a friend, he was received "with public joy, as a champion that had defied the King of his own court."

At home John was told by Elizabeth that she had secured for him an offer of a "place of honour and profit" worth about £1,000 a year. To Elizabeth's "extraordinary griefe," he re-fused the offer. He said he preferred to fight for eight pence a day till he saw the liberties and peace of England settled than to set himself down in a rich place for his own advantage.

"I scorned to be so base as to sit down in a whole skin, to make myself rich, while the liberties and freedomes of the king-dome was in danger," he explained in one of his many pamph-lets.

He returned to the army a few weeks later, this time as a major of foot soldiers. Elizabeth and their small son went with him and for a while lived in quarters at Boston, about a hundred miles north of London. There Lilburne was close to Oliver Cromwell, who, he thought at that time, had a spirit for freedom akin to his own. About a year later, as a lieutenant-colonel of dragoons, or mounted infantry, he took an important part in the victory of Marston Moor. He was shot through the arm in a minor battle a month later.

In the spring of 1645 Lilburne was faced with a weighty matter of conscience. In return for the military aid they were giving, the Scots had demanded that soldiers of the Parliamentary army should make a covenant to preserve the Scottish religion and to remodel the English religion "according to the word of God," by which the Scots meant Presbyterianism. Because Lilburne believed that each man should be free to choose his own religion, he would not subscribe to the covenant. He therefore resigned from the army on April 30, 1645, after nearly three years of service. His resignation ended chapter five of his life but not his troubles.

FAMILY MAN AND PAMPHLETEER

The year 1645, in which Lieutenant-Colonel John Lilburne left the Parliamentary army and went to live with his family in Halfe-moone Alley, Westminster, was of great importance to him and to England. Parliamentary victories at Naseby and elsewhere had increased the importance of Cromwell and almost put an end to the fighting. Differences between Puritan sects, for example the Presbyterians and the Independents, became more pronounced. Dr. Bastwick and other Puritan friends of earlier years became Lilburne's enemies.

Parliament, having defeated the king's forces, had adopted some of the oppressive measures that had caused the war. The Star Chamber had been abolished, but a Committee of Examinations had been established by Parliament in early 1643 to search for printing presses engaged in "scandalous" printing, to destroy such presses, and to commit to prison all printers and others involved. An ordinance later in the year provided that no book was to be printed unless entered in the register of the Stationers' Company.

While still in the army Lilburne had been called before the Committee of Examinations and questioned about two of his letters that had been published as pamphlets by an unlicensed press. For remarks he had made publicly less than three months after he left the army he was again called before the committee and accused of slander against the Speaker of the House of Commons. Because he knew the writings of Sir Edward Coke almost as well as the Bible, he was well versed in the law of the land.

He challenged the right of the committee to question him. He pointed out that the committee was acting as a court and therefore illegally. He referred to Magna Carta.

"I build upon the Grand Charter of England," he declared. "I have as true a right to all the priviledges that doe belong to a freeman, as the greatest man in England."

He then started reading aloud from Magna Carta. When he was told to leave the room, he strode away, reading Magna Carta to his jailer.

The following day the Committee of Examinations had good reason to become angry. A pamphlet was being circulated in the streets of London. Printed by an unlicensed printer, *Copy of a Letter from Lieutenant-Colonel John Lilburne to a friend* was Lilburne's account of his appearance before the committee. In it he called members of Parliament persecutors of religion other than their own. He accused them of setting up illegal courts, of having persuaded people to fight in the name of freedom for what was tyranny in a new form, of living in luxury while women who had lost their husbands, and children who had lost their fathers, were living in want.

In August Lilburne was again called before the Commit-

tee of Examinations. Demanding justice in accordance with
Magna Carta, a crowd followed him to the door of the hearing room. The committee ignored the crowd and ordered Lilburne to Newgate Prison. The House of Commons confirmed
the order.

Holding to the same ideals of liberty for which he had
fought, Lilburne was now a prisoner of Parliament as he had
been a prisoner of King Charles. The army owed him a large
amount of back pay. The occupation for which he had been
trained, wholesale cloth merchant, was closed to him because
of a monopoly by the Merchants Adventurers, a powerful trad-
ing company. His religious liberty was threatened by Presbyterians, who were then dominant in Parliament and were the
principal rivals of the Independents, the sect to which Lilburne
belonged.

"And after I see I was rob'd of my trade," he wrote, "and
in greater bondage by my fighting for justice, liberty, and
freedome, then I was before: I was at a mighty stand with
myselfe what to do to provide for my selfe and family."

After being kept in prison for two months Lilburne was
released, possibly because Parliament realized that if it brought
him to trial it would be giving him a public platform for appealing to the common people. He returned to his home in
Halfe-moone Alley, where his wife was expecting another child.
There he became one of the most active leaders of the radical
Independents, whose high hopes, similar to his own, the war
had failed to satisfy and who were gradually forming a political party which would eventually be known as the Levellers.

At about the time Lilburne was released from Newgate
Prison, a fifty-page pamphlet, *Englands Birth-right justified*,
appeared in the London streets. Written mainly by Lilburne,
the pamphlet called for observance of the rule of law. It stated

that the end of the war had left the lives, laws, and liberties of the people still in danger. It advocated observance of the laws by king, Parliament, and subjects alike, and asked that the laws be translated from Latin and Old French into English so that all free men could read them.

To be legal, the pamphlet specified, a trial must consist of a charge set forth in the English language in accordance with known laws, and the accused must be at liberty to make his defense. Nor should any man be required to incriminate himself.

Monopolies should be abolished, the pamphlet maintained —monopolies of trade, preaching, and printing. Elections to Parliament should be held each year, and members who were poor should be paid. Government officials suspected of wrongdoing should be tried and, if found guilty, punished. Taxation should be revised to make the burden fall more heavily on the rich than on the poor; tithing should be abolished. The charters of cities should be published so that citizens would know their provisions.

The pamphlet outlined a program too large to be accomplished in a few years by a group as small as the radical Independents, even when led by a person having the energy of John Lilburne. But the ideas expressed have echoed and re-echoed down the years, and some of them are found in the Declaration of Independence and the Constitution of the United States, particularly in the first ten amendments, or Bill of Rights.

In February 1646 the House of Lords declared the sentence that had been imposed on Lilburne by the Star Chamber eight years before was "illegal, and most unjust, against the liberty of the Subject, and the Law of the Land, and Magna Carta." But five months later this same House charged Lilburne with "High Crimes and Misdemeanors done and committed by him." The high crimes and misdemeanors consisted of writing and publishing *The Freemans Freedome vindicated* and several other pamphlets critical of the House of Lords.

Three times Lilburne was called before the bar of the august House of Lords. The first time he refused to kneel. The second time he plugged his ears with his fingers to keep from hearing the charges read against him. The third time he loudly proclaimed that he had appealed his case to the House of Commons and would stand by his appeal as long as he lived.

The House of Lords pronounced Lilburne guilty of the original charges against him and added a further charge, high contempt of the honor of the House. It sentenced him to a fine of £2,000 and imprisonment in the Tower of London for as long as the House wished to keep him there. It disqualified him from ever again holding office, military or civil, and enjoined that he not "contrive, publish, or spread any seditious or libellous Pamphlets against both or either of the Houses of Parliament." No one was to speak to him except in the presence of the keeper. If his wife wished to see him, she would have to live in the Tower with him and not be allowed to go in and out of the prison.

Separation from Elizabeth was so great a tribulation that John requested the House of Lords to allow her to join him, for "my wife is all the earthly comfort that now in this world I have left unto me. . . . And truly . . . God hath so knit in affection, the hearts and soules of me and my wife, and made us so willing to help to bear one another's burdens, that I professe, as in the sight of God, I had rather you should immediately beat out my braiens, then deprive me of the society of my wife."

[*69*]

His request was granted, and Elizabeth went to live with him in the infamous prison.

The following October and again in November Lilburne was called before the committee appointed by the House of Commons to examine him. At the hearings he complained bitterly of his treatment before the House of Lords. After the hearings, he was given pen, ink, and paper for writing a report. The report was not only delivered to the chairman of the committee, as required, but a few days later, to the surprise of Parliament, it was being circulated in London as a pamphlet printed by an unknown press, *An Anatomy of the Lords Tyranny and injustice exercised upon Lieut. Col. John Lilburne, now a Prisoner in the Tower.*

Lilburne was to spend most of the remainder of his life in prison or in exile, but he continued to fight for human rights and liberties. He even enlarged his concerns to include the improvement of prison conditions, reform of city governments, improved living conditions for the poor, and just rights for the common soldier in the army.

All efforts of Parliament to keep Lilburne from communicating with the outside world were failures. He continued to write pamphlets and to have them smuggled out and published, and he had frequent communication with other men who believed as he did, both those in the army and those out of it.

Lilburne and his friends (and most other radical Independents) believed that man was born free and with certain natural rights. They wanted to abolish the practice of special privilege, whether political, social, or economic. Because they believed in equality before the law, they demanded that all men have the right to vote. Some of them excluded beggars and servants, perhaps because the votes of such persons could be easily controlled by others. They demanded a written constitution that should embody three rights they considered inalienable: life, liberty, and property. They believed that the only existing laws that were justified were those based on reason.

"If it be not reason," Lilburne wrote, "the pronunciation of 10,000 judges cannot make it law." And "no government can be just or durable but what is founded and established upon the principles of right reason, common and universal justice, equity and conscience."

In early 1647 a large petition addressed to Parliament was circulated throughout London. Clearly reflecting the influence of John Lilburne, the petition included demands for freedom of conscience, freedom of speech, freedom of the press, the reform of city government and of prison management, the abolition of monopolies, parliamentary reform, and social legislation to benefit the poor. The government confiscated the petition.

By this time King Charles I had been handed over by the Scots to the English and was a prisoner of the Parliamentary forces at Holmby House, not far from Oxford. Fighting had stopped, and Parliament was preparing to disband its army; some of its units were as well known for their piety as for their excellent fighting ability.

Looking at events from his prison in the Tower, Lilburne was now convinced that Parliament had become as oppressive as King Charles and his Royalist government had been. He saw the army as a moral force and the only military force strong enough to stand up against Parliament and the London militia it controlled. From the Tower he appealed to the common people "to keep the Army on foot, for your owne defence, and preservation of your selves, your estates, and liberties."

He wrote a letter to Oliver Cromwell, then a powerful

member of the House of Commons, appealing to him to turn from evil advisers. "O Cromwell thou art led by the nose by two unworthy covetous earthworms." He asked how officers and men of the army could lay down their arms "before they see the lawes and universall well known liberties of England fairly settled."

He sent the letter to Cromwell by his wife, Elizabeth, "the gravest, wisest, and fittest messenger" he could think of, "and though a Feminine, yet of a gallant and true masculine spirit."

From the Tower he continued to direct a movement, already begun among radical Independents, that made the Parliamentary army unlike any other army before or since. Cavalrymen and foot soldiers were supplied with copies of Lilburne's pamphlets. They read and discussed them around their campfires. As civilians, some of the men had been eager readers of Lilburne's writings. Some of them had known Lilburne in the army. Most of them readily agreed with him on liberty of conscience: they believed that every man might hold and speak in matters of religion and politics as he pleased. They talked of state democracy as well as church democracy.

In each unit of the army, first in the cavalry and then in the infantry, common soldiers elected agents or adjutators (usually spelled agitators) to represent them. The agents formed a Council of Agitators, which was to consider what was fit to be done, and what was not, and to give their orders accordingly. They were to consider, also, the orders and votes of Parliament, to exercise a general power over all, and to set up a new form of government in the army.

Agents in the various units were in almost constant communication with each other, and many of them had frequent contacts with Lilburne, confined though he was in the Tower.

Some of the commissioned officers (principally those of low rank) were involved in the movement, soon to be derisively dubbed Leveller. Many were at least sympathetic toward its ideals. Officers who tried to interfere with the agents were sometimes given a hard time by the men. In one regiment the men forced their dissenting officers to dismount and give up their horses and arms.

Two immediate objectives of the agents, or agitators, were to prevent the disbanding of the army and to free Lilburne from prison. When Parliamentary commissioners arrived at Chelmsford in late May to disband the first regiment as scheduled, they found no regiment. Under orders from their agitators, the soldiers had taken the regimental colors and marched off toward Newmarket, where a rendezvous of infantry was to be held.

A few days later, when seven regiments of foot soldiers and six of horse were drawn up on Kentford Heath near Newmarket, a delegation of agitators presented their commanding general, Sir Thomas Fairfax, with a document, "An Humble Representation of the Dissatisfaction of the Army." When they met the following day, the soldiers unanimously agreed upon another, "The Solemne Engagement of the Armie." In the second document they pledged not to disband until its provisions had been met. One provision stipulated that the governing body of the army should no longer be the Council of War, composed entirely of officers. Rather it should be the Council of the Army, a newly created group, composed of two commissioned officers and two private soldiers elected by each regiment, together with such general officers as had stood by "The Solemne Engagement."

In the spring of 1647, to a remarkable degree the army ruled England, the agitators ruled the army, and John Lilburne, from his prison quarters in the Tower of London, ruled the agitators.

On the last day of May, however, a challenge to the power of the agitators and the influence of Lilburne was set in motion at a house in London. Oliver Cromwell, hero of the Civil War and still a member of the House of Commons, met with a few friends at his home in Drury Lane. Four days later he rejoined the army as a lieutenant-general. Within a month agitators were complaining to Lilburne that Cromwell and his son-in-law, Henry Ireton, were trying to break "The Solemne Engagement of the Armie."

On July 1 Lilburne wrote to Cromwell that "you have rob'd, by your unjust subtiltie, and shifting trickes the honest and gallant agitators, of all their power and authority, and solely placed it in a thing called a Counsell of Warre, or rather a Cabinet Junto of seven or eight proud selfe ended fellowes, that so you can without controule make up your owne ends."

In the summer of 1647, the radical Independents formally withdrew from the regular Independents, and their enemies soon bestowed on them the name Levellers.

Early in August, after Lilburne had rejected the pleas of many agitators to escape from the Tower and lead a revolt, the army marched into London. As Lilburne listened to the tramp, tramp of clouted shoes and the ring of shod hoofs passing the Tower he must have thought that soon he would be free. But even in the presence of the army Parliament continued unwilling to free Lilburne—and others like him who had criticized it. Disagreement between the high officers, or grandees, and the agitators was growing. In a pamphlet Lilburne advised the agitators and other common soldiers to "trust your great officers . . . no farther than you can throw an Oxe!"

A month after the army had entered London, Lieutenant-

General Cromwell went to the Tower in the line of duty to inspect the ordnance. During his visit, he saw and talked with Lilburne, who had several times requested a meeting.

Cromwell asked Lilburne why he had fallen out with men who had once been his best friends and why he had become such a bitter enemy of Parliament. If Lilburne would be patient, Parliament would correct its errors, Cromwell said.

Lilburne denied that he had fallen out with his friends. He said they had fallen away from him and the principles for which they had once stood. He reminded Cromwell that Parliament had committed him to prison without trial. As a result, his wife and children, as well as he, had suffered greatly. All he asked was a fair trial. The oppressions of Parliament, he said, were greater than those of King Charles.

Cromwell maintained that acts of oppression had been a habit with King Charles. He justified similar acts by Parliament as matters of necessity and said that, in time, they would be corrected.

Then he admitted that Lilburne's release from the Tower had been delayed because of the fear that he would go to the army and "make new hurley-burleys there." If Lilburne would promise to be quiet, he would be released. Lilburne reluctantly promised that he would leave England for twelve months if he were given £2,ooo, which had been awarded him by Parliament as Star Chamber reparations, and half the pay the army still owed him.

"Well," said Cromwell, according to a report by Lilburne, "though you have given me little encouragement, yet such is the affection I beare you, as you shall see I will not be wanting in my best endeavours to procure your liberty of the Parliament, whereof I hope you shall find the effects in a very short time."

Then the two men dined with the lieutenant of the Tower. Lilburne took advantage of the occasion to complain about the treatment of the prisoners.

Day followed day, and Lilburne remained in the Tower. Cromwell was slow in presenting Lilburne's case to Parliament and permitted delay after delay until Lilburne was close to physical exhaustion from prison life and the daily deferment of hope for his release from the Tower.

Disillusioned by the results of the Civil War, Lilburne considered the restoration of King Charles to the throne. He even planned to have some of his friends meet with the king. Now, he believed, the king was more likely than Parliament to guard the people's rights.

Lilburne's near exhaustion did not prevent his engineering the election of new agitators in the army to replace those Cromwell had begun to influence. Exhausted or not, he was faced with another hearing before a committee of the House of Commons, which he hoped would release him from prison. Early in November, perhaps because of his ill health, he was granted liberty on bail to leave the Tower daily during daylight hours to prepare his defense.

Surprisingly, John Lilburne had little or no active part in the actual writing of two of the most important documents of the period. Preparing for his hearing before the committee and supervising the newly elected agitators occupied most of his time. But the two documents clearly showed the influence of Lilburne upon the men who wrote them, the result of his ten years of working on the minds of other men. Both documents were designed to guarantee representative government and to protect the people from oppression by the persons they elected to represent them.

The first of these documents, written mainly or entirely

by agitators, became known as "The Case of the Armie." It was completed on October 9, 1647. Its full title suggests its history as well as its contents: "The Case of the Armie Truly Stated, together with the mischiefes and dangers that are imminent, and some sutable remedies, Humbly proposed by the Agents of five regiments of horse to their respective regiments and the whole Army."

This document started with typical soldierly complaints, such as arrears in pay, and ended with demands for rights that should be enjoyed by all free-born men, soldiers and civilians alike. It concluded with a demand for suffrage: "All the free-born at the age of twenty-one years and upwards [should] be the electors." (Some exceptions were mentioned.)

It was signed by eleven agents or agitators and handed to their commanding general with a letter. The writers of the letter declared they had acted from "obligations upon our consciences (written naturally by the finger of God in our hearts)." They added that "God hath given no man a talent to be wrapped up in a napkin and not improved, but the meanest vassal (in the eye of the world) is equally obliged, and accomptable to God, with the greatest prince or commander under the sun in and for the use of that talent betrusted unto him."

The second document, written by one of Lilburne's civilian friends with the help of army agents and possibly Lilburne, was "An Agreement of the People." As with the other document, its full title suggests both its history and its contents: "An Agreement of the People for a firme and present peace, upon grounds of common-right and freedome; As it was proposed by the Agents of the five regiments of horse; and since by the generall approbation of the Army, offered to the joynt concurrence of all the free Commons of England."

[77]

"An Agreement of the People" contained many ideas from "The Case of the Army." As published on November 3, 1647, it included four important reforms: the establishment of electoral districts having approximately equal numbers of inhabitants; the dissolution of the present Parliament; the election of new Parliaments every second year; and a definition of the power of Parliament, which was to be inferior only to the power of the electors.

It provided for freedom of religion. It declared that the impressing or drafting of men "to serve in the wars is against our freedom." It specified that all persons are to be equal before the law. It contained the statement that "as the laws ought to be equal, so they must be good, and not evidently destructive to the safety and well-being of the people."

The basic ideas for "An Agreement of the People" were the law of nature and the law of reason. Neither law was new. But Lilburne and other Levellers had given expression to them in ways that spoke to the Englishmen of their time. Acceptance of these laws led to a belief in man's natural and inalienable rights, rights that were to be proclaimed again, three thousand miles across the Atlantic, at the time of the American Revolution. The rights of one man are the rights of all men, the Levellers believed. The good of the people is the highest law, said the Levellers in English, and, in Latin, *Salus populi suprema lex.*

If accepted, the "Agreement" would become the basis for a national written constitution. The idea of an agreement or contract between the leader and the led was not new to the people of England. They had read that in biblical times Jehovah had made a contract or covenant with his people. They knew that English kings, when they were crowned, were assumed to have made contracts with their subjects. And they had Magna Carta.

On October 28 the Council of the Army met in the parish church at Putney, the army headquarters on the south bank of the Thames near London, to discuss both documents. The discussion turned into bitter debates, mainly over "An Agreement of the People," that lasted until November 11. On one side were Lieutenant-General Oliver Cromwell; his son-in-law, Henry Ireton, a skillful debater; and others who held that only men of property or men with annual incomes above a certain amount should be allowed to vote. On the other side were men who, like Lilburne, believed the franchise should not be based on property or income. Most of these were agitators or common soldiers. A few were officers who believed with Colonel William Rainsborough, an eloquent advocate of the Leveller position, that "the poorest hee that is in England hath a life to live as the greatest hee."

Lilburne was not at the debates in the Council of the Army at Putney. He was still confined to the Tower of London or out on bail in the neighborhood.

During the debates Cromwell derisively referred to his opponents as Levellers. He said that they wanted "to level Men of all Qualities and Estates," that is, to level or make equal all men socially and economically as well as politically and legally. His opponents objected to the name. They said it was inaccurate. But it stuck to them, and soon all men and women who believed as they and Lilburne did were called Levellers, even though they advocated social and economic reform and not social and economic leveling.

At the end of the Putney debates the Levellers appeared by their votes to have won. Their proposal that the "Agreement" should be submitted to the people of England for approval or disapproval was carried, as was a motion for a general rendezvous of the army at which the "Agreement" would be submitted to the soldiers. Agitators present at the debates reported to their regiments that the proposal for manhood suffrage without property or income qualification was carried with only three negative votes.

Cromwell strongly opposed manhood suffrage and equal electoral districts; he declared "that the first particular of that which they called the Agreement of the People did tend very much to anarchy."

Lieutenant-General Cromwell had a rank and a reputation that were often more persuasive than words. He carried a vote in the Council of the Army that the rendezvous should be held in three phases on three different days, the first on November 15. The separate meetings would make mutiny, if it occurred, easier to handle. He carried another vote that all agitators and officers present should be sent back to their regiments at once.

At the first rendezvous, at Corkbush Field near Ware, the men of two regiments who were not ordered to be there marched onto the field. They had driven away many of their officers and were led chiefly by their agitators. Each soldier had a copy of *An Agreement of the People* stuck in his hat. Plainly visible in bold letters on each pamphlet were the words "England's Freedom-Soldiers' Rights." By their very presence the regiments were guilty of mutiny.

At the sight of the pamphlets Cromwell bluntly ordered the soldiers to take them from their hats. When the men of one regiment refused to obey, Cromwell angrily rode among them, snatching the pamphlets. Overawed by the victorious general whom for three years they had followed in battle, the men did not resist. By Cromwell's orders several leaders among the soldiers were immediately tried for mutiny, and three were sentenced to death. One of the boldest, Richard Arnold, was executed by a firing squad before the assembled regiments.

CHALLENGER OF CROMWELL

With the death of Arnold and the end of the mutiny at Corkbush Field, the seventh chapter in the life of John Lilburne began. It was a new phase in the struggle between Lilburne and Cromwell, two men who were alternately generous friends and bitter enemies. Cromwell won because he had the power and the will to use it. Lilburne was to learn that the army, as well as the king and Parliament, could be tyrannical.

Yet even in defeat Lilburne had his temporary victories and his hours of glory. More important, to the end of his life he held to his ideals.

On November 9, 1647, "An Agreement of the People," crammed with Lilburne's ideas and ideals, was declared by the House of Commons to be "destructive to the Being of Parliaments, and to the fundamental Government of the Kingdom." Although it was later rewritten several times, no version of it was ever "offered to the joynt concurrence of all the free Commons of England," that is, submitted to popular vote. But many of the ideas and ideals it expressed were carried in the minds and hearts of hundreds of the English people who sailed three thousand miles overseas to build small, new Englands on the North American continent.

As a result of a petition containing more than eight thousand signatures and an eloquent speech in the House of Commons by Sir John Maynard, a Presbyterian who had shared a period of imprisonment in the Tower with John Lilburne, the two houses of Parliament voted to release Lilburne. After two years in prison Lilburne was freed on August 2, 1648. At the time Cromwell was out of London fighting the second civil war against a Royalist army. The fleet had recently gone Royalist.

King Charles had escaped to the Isle of Wight. The nation was suffering from high taxes, depressed economic conditions, and widespread hunger resulting from poor crops. Cromwell had many enemies in and about London. The enemies wondered whether Lilburne would join them. He would not.

The day after his release from the Tower Lilburne sent Cromwell a letter by a faithful friend. "Assure your self that if ever my hand be upon you, it shall be when you are in your full glory, if then you shall decline from the righteous wayes of Truth and Justice: Which, if you will fixedly and impartially prosecute, I am Yours, to the last drop of my heart bloud (for all your late severe hand towards me)."

Although Lilburne scorned to strike when Cromwell was beset by other foes, he still feared the power that Cromwell and the army had attained. Without a king or a truly representative Parliament, the people would be left to the "wills and swords" of the army and would be ruled over "arbitrarily, without declared Laws, as a conquered people."

After the second civil war ended in 1648, Lilburne agreed with Cromwell and the army that King Charles should be tried. But he believed that, first, a new government should be established. A new and truly representative Parliament should be elected in accordance with a revised version of "An Agreement of the People." Neither the army nor the present Parliament, which had been purged of all members not approved by the army, had a right to try the king.

And the king should be tried by established law, Lilburne maintained, rather than by the High Court of Justice created by the purged Parliament. Was the king to be tried for murder? The established law laid down procedures in a trial for murder and made no exceptions for king, queen, or prince. Had the king, with his own hands, committed murder? The law held the instigator of murder as guilty as the actual perpetrator. The questions were hypothetical. The answers were expressions of broad principles that applied to everyone.

John Lilburne and his brother Robert were invited to sit as judges at the trial of King Charles. Robert accepted. John refused. He journeyed north to his old home at Thickley Punchardon in Durham and spent the time of the trial there. He disapproved of the trial, the sentence, and the execution of the king, who was convicted of high treason against the Parliamentary forces.

Returning to London disillusioned, John resolved to devote himself to the well-being of his wife and children. Two of his children—one was named Tower—had been born while he was in prison. The family took rooms in Winchester House, a large apartment building, once a home of bishops, later a prison.

Offered a government job, Lilburne refused it. To accept, he felt, would be to support an unjust and illegal Parliament. The fame of his skill in court had spread, and he was often asked for legal aid. Among those he counseled were five Royalists being tried before the specially created High Court of Justice. Lilburne maintained that the court was illegal.

The execution of King Charles brought no relief to common soldiers in the army. In early February 1649 they presented the rump Parliament with a petition for their back pay, abolition of tithes, legal reform, and provision for the poor. The petition was for their families as well as for themselves. They asked not to be ordered to infringe on civilian rights— for example, not ordered to seize unlicensed books or printing presses. They demanded reinstatement of the Council of the Army, with agitators representing the common soldiers.

Cromwell and the other high officers were incensed. They

suspected that some evil and scandalous persons not in the army were responsible for the soldiers' attitude as expressed by the petition. They demanded from Parliament powers to punish by martial law any civilians who tried to breed discontent in the army.

When Lilburne learned of their demand, he forgot his resolve to devote himself to the support of his family. In late February he went to the House of Commons and stood at the bar, a free man, where he had once stood a prisoner. After a short and, for him, restrained speech he presented the House with a copy of his latest pamphlet, *Englands New Chains Discovered*, which was sharply critical of the government. He covered in the pamphlet all his old grievances—interference with the press, imprisonment for debt, monopolies, tithing, and other injustices. He also called for the dissolution of the Council of State, headed by Cromwell.

Less than a month later he wrote and published *Englands New Chains Discovered, Part II*. In it he accused Cromwell and the other grandees of seeking power and domination for themselves. He called for a truly representative government, less burdensome taxes, and a free press. On March 24 he read his pamphlet to a large and enthusiastic crowd in front of Winchester House. Then he carried it to the House of Commons. The crowd followed. Without much delay the House declared the pamphlet to be "highly seditious, and destructive to the present Government." It pronounced the author guilty of high treason.

Four days later, between four and five in the morning, more than a hundred horse and foot soldiers besieged Winchester House. Some of them battered their way into Lilburne's apartment, took Lilburne prisoner, and marched him through the London streets to St. Paul's Cathedral. There

Lilburne found two of his Leveller friends and later, at White-hall, another. All were prisoners, and their arrests had been as violent as his.

Before the end of the day each of the four prisoners was brought before the Council of State, presided over by Crom-well. Lilburne protested that the council had no power to try him. He objected to the Star Chamber methods of questioning and refused to answer. He is reported to have told the council, "I know not what you intend to do with me, neither do I much care; having learned long since to dy, and rather for my Liberties, than in my bed."

Lilburne and his three friends were committed to the Tower of London on suspicion of treason. In his account of the event Lilburne wrote, "So now I have brought the Reader to my old and contented Lodging in the Tower."

During the next two months several petitions for the release of the four men were carried to the House of Commons from nearby districts as well as London. The presentation of each petition was the occasion for a demonstration of Levellers, men and women, wearing their sea-green emblems. Two of the April petitions were said to have had more than ten thousand signatures each.

London newspapers printed reports of "the bonny Besses in the sea-green dresses" and their petitions for "honest John o' the Tower." When members of the House of Commons told women petitioners that the matter at hand was of "higher concernment than they understood," and to go home and look after "their huswifry," the women responded with a small riot. With their tongues they "pelted hail-shot against the Members as they passed to and fro." The women seized one member and would not release him until he swore he was for the liberties of the people.

Even in the Tower Lilburne and his three friends continued to write pamphlets that were smuggled out to be printed and distributed. On May 1, 1649, after they had sat "close in councell every day" for several weeks, they issued what they hoped would be the final version of "An Agreement of the People." The civil wars had been caused by uncertain government and arbitrary power, the four men asserted. Adoption of the "Agreement" should mean that government would be certain, known, and bounded.

Although Lilburne and three other prominent Levellers were imprisoned in the Tower, Cromwell did not feel secure. He feared Lilburne even in prison because of "such discontents and mutinies as are dayly contracted in the Army by meanes of his Seditious scribling."

Discontent among the soldiers over low pay and other unsatisfactory conditions in the army, and over the threat of being sent to fight in Ireland, had become acute. A mutiny that occurred in London in 1649 was led by twenty-three-year-old Robert Lockier, a Leveller and an agitator who had been in the army since he was sixteen. He was known as "a pious man, and of excellent parts, and much beloved." On a day in late April, about sixty men of a cavalry troop, with Lockier at their head, seized the regimental colors, barricaded themselves in the Bull Inn in Bishopsgate Street, and vowed not to come out until they had been promised improvement in their army conditions.

Soon after Cromwell learned of the mutiny, he was at the inn. Fifteen troopers were taken into custody. The others escaped or had previously submitted to their officers.

Of the fifteen taken into custody, Lockier and five others were sentenced by a court martial to be executed. On petitions for mercy, the five were pardoned. When Lockier learned that his petition had been rejected, he denounced the court that tried him as tyrannical.

Lilburne learned of the court martial and joined with other London citizens in an appeal for Lockier's reprieve. Lockier himself signed the appeal. When it was ignored, he made no further appeal and no complaint.

He was taken to St. Paul's for the execution on Friday, April 27, the day after his conviction. His sisters and cousins were there. He spoke cheerfully to them and to others nearby.

Then he turned and, as recorded by one of those present, spoke to the firing squad: "I did not think that you had such heathenish and barbarous principles in you, as to obey your Officers in murthering of me, when I stand up for nothing but what is for your good."

When he was asked if he wanted to have his eyes covered, he replied that his cause was so just that he did not fear to face death.

His last words were to the crowd of bystanders: "I pray you, let not this death of mine be a discouragement, but rather an incouragement; for never man died more comfortably than I do."

Like Richard Arnold, Lockier "died a very Martyr for the Liberties of England." He was given the funeral honors of a general by Levellers and their friends. About a thousand soldiers walked slowly before the hearse. On the coffin rested the dead soldier's naked sword; his horse, draped in black, walked behind. Lockier's relatives and more than two thousand citizens and soldiers marched behind the horse. At the churchyard waited many more.

The occasion was orderly and without disturbance. It was a ceremony of consecration. It was also an occasion "to let Cromwell and Fairfax both know . . . that this is not the way

[*87*]

to crush the Free People of this Nation," for other troubles among the regiments, particularly among those assigned to service in Ireland, soon followed the execution of Lockier.

In May mutinies occurred simultaneously at Salisbury and Banbury. Cromwell ended the Banbury mutiny by a surprise midnight attack on the battle-weary mutineers at nearby Burford, where the mutineers were spending the night. He captured four hundred of them. Several hundred escaped. The captured men were imprisoned in the Burford church while the Council of War decided their fate. The next day they were led out of the church to watch three of their leaders shot against the west wall of the churchyard.

The Banbury-Burford incident acted as a stimulus to both Cromwell and Lilburne. In a great fury Cromwell declared that Lilburne was responsible for the mutiny. Pounding on a table, he swore in the presence of his officers that either Lilburne or he should die for it. Determined that he should not be the one to die, he decided to bring Lilburne to trial.

Lilburne responded to the incident by writing a pamphlet that the government considered shockingly seditious, *An Impeachment of High Treason against Oliver Cromwell and his Son in Law Henry Ireton.* Although he completed the pamphlet in July, he held up its publication until August 10, because his wife, daughter, and two sons had become ill from smallpox. Both boys died, but his wife and daughter recovered. The death of his two sons, he wrote, was "a greater tryal of my dependence upon God, then ever I had in my life."

In September of 1649 a summons for trial was served on Lilburne. Before eight sober judges in the crowded guildhall he was charged on October 24 with high treason under two recent acts of Parliament. Among the charges were that through his writings he tried to disturb the peace of the nation by declaring the government to be unlawful and tyrannical; he did "maliciously, advisedly, and traiterously . . . plot, contrive and endeavour to stir up and to raise force" against the government; and "as a false Traytour did maliciously, advisedly and Trayterously indeavour to stir up a dangerous mutinous, and Trayterous distemper, Mutiny and Rebellion in the Army."

Included as government evidence were the *Impeachment of High Treason against Oliver Cromwell* and four other pamphlets Lilburne was accused of having written.

Fully aware that he was on trial for his life, Lilburne called up all the legal knowledge and skill he had learned over the years. He was allowed no counsel or lawyer to argue his case for him. He challenged each point brought up by the prosecutor. Claiming that his trial was illegal, he pointed out that he was being tried under two acts passed after his arrest and original charge. As usual, he was convinced that in fighting for his rights he was fighting for the rights of all Englishmen.

During most of the trial the judges were patient with Lilburne, his objections, and his arguments. They knew that he had many friends in and out of the courtroom—so many outside that soldiers had been called to keep order. Perhaps because they saw that his friends in the courtroom outnumbered the others about twenty to one, they were restrained in warning against the outbursts of friends in the room.

On the second day of the trial, after standing for five hours defending himself, Lilburne asked for a day or even a few hours to rest and to organize his final argument. The judges refused his request. They told him he must clear himself at once of the charge of writing the pamphlets.

"Then," shouted Lilburne, "I appeale to the righteous God of heaven and earth against you!"

His shouted reply to the judges was followed by a much

louder reply—a reply that even he could not have anticipated or engineered—a deafening roar as temporary scaffolding in the courtroom splintered and crashed to the floor.

After order was restored, the trial continued, and at last Lilburne faced the jury for his final plea. He appealed to the jurors as fellow citizens: "Therefore, you Gentlemen of the Jury, my sole Judges, the keepers of my life . . . I desire you to know your power, and consider your duty, both to God, to Me, to your own Selves, and to your Country; and the gracious assisting Spirit, the presence of the Lord God omnipotent, the Governor of Heaven and Earth, and all things therein contained, go along with you, give counsell, and direct you, to do that which is just and for his glory."

Lilburne's friends in the courtroom shouted "Amen! Amen!" and made so much noise that the judges feared violent disorder. Outside, three more companies of foot soldiers were sent for.

An hour after the jury retired at five o'clock, the court reassembled.

The dramatic courtroom scene has been preserved by a spectator who left this record from shorthand notes he made at the trial.

> "Are you agreed of your verdict?" asked the Clerk.
>
> "Yes."
>
> "Who shall speak for you?"
>
> "Our Fore-man."
>
> "John Lilburn, hold up thy hand, what say you, look upon the Prisoner, is he guilty of the Treasons, charged upon him: or any of them, or not guilty?"
>
> "Not guilty of all of them."
>
> "Nor of all the Treason, or any of them that are layed to his charge?"
>
> "No, of all, nor of any of them."
>
> The juryman's "No!" being pronounced in a very loud voice,

immediately the whole multitude of People in the Hall, for joy of the prisoner's acquittal gave such a loud and unanimous shout, as is beleeved, was never heard in Yeeld-Hall, which lasted for about halfe an hour without intermission: which made the Judges for fear, turne pale, and hange down their heads; but the Prisoner stood silent at the Barre, rather more sad in his countenance than he was before.

An engraving made by a contemporary artist shows Lilburne at this first trial for his life. A man somewhat taller than average and apparently well muscled is fashionably dressed in a buttoned jacket, with lace collar and cuffs, short trousers with a bottom fringe and decorative side slashes, and conspicuous boots with large roweled spurs. He wears a small mustache, and tousled hair falls to his shoulders. His face, reflecting the hardships of war, prison, and the bitter struggle for human rights, is mature for his approximately thirty-four years.

Although acquitted by the court, Lilburne was taken back to the Tower. Shouting and cheering, hundreds of admirers followed him. Even the soldiers who guarded him were "hollowing and shouting as they Rid in the streets for joy at his deliverance." Some of them shot their pistols and blew their trumpets. At night people lighted bonfires to celebrate their hero's acquittal. When Lilburne and three other Levellers were released from prison two weeks later, a huge crowd marched in companies to a celebration feast at the King's Head Tavern in Fish Street.

Fighting in Ireland at the time, Cromwell was enraged and puzzled at the news of Lilburne's acquittal. For Lilburne the acquittal was a splendid personal victory, but it did not help his cause. In the months and years that followed, steady pressure from Cromwell caused the influence of the Levellers to decline.

For about a year and a half after his acquittal Lilburne was unnaturally docile. He wrote no controversial pamphlets. He was elected common councillor in the London city elections in late 1649 but was denied his office on a technicality.

A period of friendly relations between Lilburne and Cromwell followed the general's return to London in May 1650 from his bloody conquest of Ireland. Cromwell used his influence to get a grant of land for the man who, less than a year before, he had tried to get hanged for high treason. Lilburne, in a spirit of friendship and gratitude, rode the first twenty-five miles in a military campaign of the man who, less than a year before, he had tried to get impeached for high treason. A few months later Lilburne wrote Cromwell of his "reall graitfull acknowledgment of your Excilencys most obliging and nobell favours manifested unto myselfe." Still later Lilburne visited Cromwell at his London home, and the two men talked for a while, cordially and alone.

Remembering his resolve to give more time to the support of his family, Lilburne took up soap-making. Another son, John, had been born in October 1650, and the family needed money.

The drab, messy business of soap-making did not fit a nervous temperament. Lilburne neglected and finally abandoned it to give more time to the many persons who came to him seeking legal advice. Hoping to improve his service to clients, he applied for admission to the Inner Temple, one of the societies controlling the practice of law. He was not admitted. Monopoly existed in the law as well as in other professions and trades.

The law and a pamphlet combined to bring John Lilburne eventually to his second trial for life. John was one of the lawyers in a case his uncle George Lilburne had brought against

Sir Arthur Haselrig, the owner of several coal mines in northern England. In the dispute over a mine Parliament's Committee of Haberdasher's Hall, which had jurisdiction over such matters, decided in favor of Sir Arthur.

Without delay John rushed into print with a pamphlet, *A Just Report of Haberdasher's Hall*, in the caustic style for which he had become famous. He accused Sir Arthur of dishonesty in dealings with his uncle and of using undue pressure to influence the committee. He prepared a petition containing the same charges. With several other persons he signed the petition and, on December 23, 1651, he presented it to Parliament.

Assuming the judicial powers often condemned in the Star Chamber, the House of Commons reacted by declaring both the pamphlet and the petition libelous and imposing a shockingly heavy fine of £7,000 on John Lilburne and one of the other signers. In addition, it banished John from England on pain of death if he should return.

The severity of the sentence in proportion to the alleged crime stunned even Lilburne, who was not allowed to speak in his defense. Later John heard through his wife that Cromwell had said the sentence would not have been made so severe if other things were not feared from him.

To make matters more difficult for Lilburne the House of Commons reduced from the original thirty to twenty the number of days it allowed him to prepare for leaving the country.

After arranging with friends to care for his wife and children, Lilburne took horse for Dover on January 29, 1652. Many of his friends rode with him for several miles. Two days later he arrived at Dover—but without a passport. It had been withheld by the Speaker of the House, possibly to ensure that he would be trapped in England after the expiration of the twenty-day limit. He was able to leave England only after the mayor of Dover's wife had burst into tears and begged that Lilburne be allowed to board ship for Ostend, Belgium. On the trip across the English Channel the man who had "set himself against Bishops, against Kings, against the House of Lords, against Generals, yea and Parliament itself" was violently seasick.

A week later Lilburne was living in Amsterdam, surrounded by Cromwell spies and Royalist exiles. Later he moved to Bruges in Belgium, where he spent much time reading Machiavelli's *The Prince,* Plutarch's *Lives,* Sir Walter Raleigh's *History of the World,* John Milton's *Defence of the People of England,* and similar writings.

In England, Elizabeth was forced to borrow money and to pawn or sell some of the family household goods. She visited John in Bruges several times. Her visits, which brought together two tense, anxious persons, were not happy occasions. On each visit, she begged John to live quietly and not to write controversial pamphlets.

John wrote little until March 1653, when he heard of growing unrest in the army against the Rump Parliament, which opposed reform. In a pamphlet, *L. Colonel John Lilburne Revived,* he urged the people of England to struggle to the death for the election of men who would defend the people's liberties and protect citizens from the "annihilating incroachments that their present Tyrannicall Riders have already made upon them."

Lilburne resolved never to see England "so long as Cromwell's most hatefull and detestable beastely Tyrannie lasteth, unlesse it be in a way to pursue him, as the grandest Tyrant and Traytor, that ever England bredd."

On April 20, 1653, Cromwell dissolved the Rump Parliament, which had exiled Lilburne, and Elizabeth hurried to Bruges to discuss the possibility of her husband's returning to England. In spite of their disagreements, in a recent letter to a friend, John had referred to Elizabeth as the helpmate "who for twelve years hath many times with a good proportion of strength and resolution, gone through so many miseries with me, with so much affection."

Unnamed authorities asked Lilburne if he would be quiet should he be allowed to return home. His answer was characteristic of him: "I am as free born as any man breathing in England (and therefore should have no more fetters than all other men put upon me)."

Elizabeth returned to England hoping she would be able to get a pass for her husband. John waited at Dunkirk and then at Calais, but no pass came. Deciding to risk his life on a personal appeal, he wrote to Cromwell and the Council of State. Then, early in the morning of June 14, he crossed by boat from Calais to Dover, took horse, and galloped away toward London. By changing to a fresh horse Elizabeth had waiting for him at Canterbury, he made the journey from Calais to his London home in a day.

At home in Little Moorfields, he penned another letter to Cromwell. But this letter was from a writer unlike the John Lilburne who had defied church, king, and Parliament. He wrote that he hoped the hard things he had said against Cromwell would be "construed to be the fruits of my highest passions when my reason was clouded, not only by my sad and most heavy sufferings, but also by the misapprehensions of your Excellencies actions and intentions." He now intended to live "quietly and submissively," "godly and peaceably," with his poor distressed family. He would be willing to serve

[95]

the Commonwealth or confine himself to private life. Later he stated that he wrote the letter to please his wife.

With a friend Elizabeth carried John's letter to the headquarters of Cromwell, by this time virtually a dictator. When she failed to gain an audience with the general, she left the letter.

On June 15 Lilburne was arrested for returning to England from exile, and a day later he was ordered by the Council of State to be confined in Newgate prison.

Petitions for Lilburne's release poured in from his personal friends, from soldiers, from women, from other admirers in London and other parts of England. Lilburne and other Levellers wrote, printed, and distributed pamphlets in his defense. "To the prejudice of his wisdom," someone commented, Cromwell refused to receive the petitions. But he promised a fair trial.

John Lilburne's third trial for his life was begun on July 13, 1653, at the Old Bailey. Closely supporting John in the courtroom were his father (to whom he was still sometimes a "griefe"), his father-in-law, other relatives, and several friends. On each day of the trial, petitions for his release were circulated outside and signed by his followers and sympathizers. Three regiments of cavalry were stationed nearby to cope with possible unruly demonstrations.

On the first day of the trial Lilburne delayed proceedings by engaging in a dispute with the judges before he would raise his hand and acknowledge his name. After the indictment was read, he asked for and was given permission to comment on it. He spoke against its "insufficiency and illegality." Then he asked for a copy of the indictment so that he could readily have the advice of his counsel in preparing his defense for the charges against him. The judges refused his request. Giving the accused a copy of the indictment was not the practice in English law courts, even in cases of such serious crimes as high treason and murder. Lilburne argued that having a copy of the indictment should be a right of all Englishmen accused of crime. He argued for hours and hours, and for hours and hours the judges refused his request. On the fourth day of the trial, the judges surrendered, finally acknowledging the correctness of Lilburne's position and setting a legal precedent for one of the precious rights of English law. This right was won for all Englishmen—and Americans, too—by the persistence and the noisy but skillful arguments of one man, John Lilburne. During the trial, Lilburne conducted his defense. Spectators applauded nearly everything he said.

At the end of four days of hearings the court adjourned until the next session. When it reassembled on August 10, the atmosphere was tense. More than six hundred men armed with pistols, daggers, and other weapons were rumored to be close by, ready to rescue Lilburne if the verdict went against him. The government responded to the rumor by posting two companies of foot soldiers near the Old Bailey and by ordering detachments of calvalry and foot soldiers to patrol nearby streets.

The court refused Lilburne's demand for a hearing on the legality of the Act of Banishment under which he was being tried. A copy of the indictment was read, and a jury was impaneled.

When Lilburne began his arguments, he aimed them at both the jurors and the spectators in the courtroom. He stated that all his mature life he had been a sufferer for and an as-serter of the rights and liberties of the freeborn people of England. He was prepared to die in defense of those rights and liberties. He hoped that what he died for would be

[97]

recorded for future generations. He continued his arguments for several days. On August 20 the court told him that he must plead to the indictment or be judged worthy of death.

"Not guilty," Lilburne replied. Then he made numerous objections to the charge against him—that the act under which he was banished was faulty, that he had never been properly indicted, that no proof had been established that he, John Lilburne, was the Lieutenant-Colonel John Lilburne named in the Act of Banishment. He had been illegally banished, he said. He had been convicted of no crime. He had not even been charged with a specific crime and brought into court where he would be allowed to defend himself.

Lilburne's main defense was centered on the Rump Parliament, which had banished him and which had since been dissolved by Cromwell. If the Parliament had been unlawful, then its banishment of him was illegal. On the other hand, if the Parliament had been lawful, then punishment should first be inflicted on Cromwell, the person who had illegally dissolved it.

In his moving plea to the jury Lilburne spoke for about two hours. He told the jurors that he had been banished even though he had been charged with no crime. He appealed to them to consider the precedent that would be set if he were to be condemned to death under the Act of Banishment. Under such an act and with such a precedent banishment and death might be the fate of anyone. By defending his rights, Lilburne told the jurors, they would be defending their own rights.

"If I die on Monday," he said, "may not the Parliament on Tuesday pass such a sentence against every one of you twelve, and upon your wives and children?"

The jury deliberated for several hours before announcing its verdict, "John Lilburne is not guilty of any crime worthy of death."

The shout of joy in the courtroom was heard by the soldiers and the crowds outside. Cheers and shouts of "Long live Lilburne!" echoed from the brick walls of nearby buildings. Soldiers beat their drums and sounded their trumpets.

But acquittal did not bring Lilburne freedom. He was taken back to the prison from which he had come. Cromwell interpreted the court decision and the rejoicing that followed as signs of the unpopularity of his government. He had members of the jury summoned before the Council of State and questioned, as if, in acquitting Lilburne, they had committed a crime. Most of the jurors were small tradesmen—one a bookbinder, one a candlemaker, at least one a cloth or clothing merchant. Accustomed to thinking independently, most of them would say only that they had acted as their consciences dictated. To avoid such independence the Council of State had future political offenders tried before the High Court of Justice, which sat without a jury.

On August 27, after the jurors had refused to change their verdict, the Council of State was ordered to "take some course for the further securing of Lieut.-Colonel John Lilburne for the peace of this Nation." Guarded by a troop of horse, Lilburne was quietly removed to the Tower at night. Elizabeth was allowed to join him there, on condition that she would not leave the prison or allow his friends to see him. Lilburne showed no interest when Cromwell was named lord protector. By January 1654 he was being permitted to have a few visitors and given an allowance of £2 a week.

Even in the Tower Lilburne was feared by Cromwell. He might be involved in Royalist or Leveller plots against the government. The lord protector and the Council of State decided that "for the public peace" Lilburne should be removed from the English mainland. On March 16, 1654, the council ordered him transferred from the Tower to a gloomy castle on the island of Jersey, where he was kept a close prisoner. Shortly after Lilburne arrived at his new prison, Elizabeth, still in London, gave birth to her ninth child.

At the age of thirty-nine or thereabouts, Lilburne was weary in mind, body, and spirit. The battle for justice and human rights in which he had spent more than fifteen strenuous years seemed lost. He was cut off completely from the crowds that stimulated and inspired him—the people for whose rights he had sacrificed his best years.

In June 1655 old Henry Dewell, Elizabeth's father, visited John in his gloomy prison. On his return to London he reported that his son-in-law protested against any way of gaining his liberty but through the law.

A month later Elizabeth and Richard Lilburne petitioned Cromwell for the release of their husband and son from the island prison in which he had already spent sixteen depressing months.

"I beg you," wrote Elizabeth, "to take away all provocation from his impatient spirit, wearied out with long and sore afflictions, and enlarge him, in pity to me and my children. I durst engage my life that he will not disturb the state. I should not else desire his liberty."

In August or September Cromwell promised Elizabeth that her husband would be brought back to England. In early October John landed at Dover harbor in a small ship loaded with hogsheads of cider. He was not a free man. But his new prison, Dover Castle, perched on the chalk cliffs, overlooked the blue of the English Channel and the green of the English countryside. It was a pleasanter prison than the gloomy Jersey castle.

John's return to England was not altogether happy.

Elizabeth, living in poverty at the home of a friend, had accepted from Sir Arthur Haselrig certain County Durham lands that her husband had maintained were rightfully his. When John, in his Dover prison, was visited by Elizabeth he quarreled with her bitterly over her acceptance of the lands. Sir Arthur could not rob him of his lands and then return some as a favor!

THE QUAKER

And then began the final chapter in the life of John Lilburne. While in his Jersey prison John had become acquainted with a Quaker, a member of the Society of Friends. At Dover he talked with other Quakers. He asked for and read Quaker writings and gave some to Elizabeth. The directness, openness, simplicity, honesty, and courage of the Quakers struck responsive chords in him.

In November his quarreling with Elizabeth stopped. On one of her visits to Dover he told her of his spiritual uneasiness. After her return to London, she wrote him that on the journey home she had nearly lost her life in an accident on the Thames. Then she added, "My Dear, Retain a sober patient Spirit within thee, which I am confident thou shalt see shall be of more force to recover thee, then all thy keen mettal hath been; I hope God is doing a work upon thee and me too, as shall make us study ourselves more then we have done."

John found a kinship with the Quaker way of bearing witness to the truth within them and in their willingness to suffer persecution and imprisonment for their outward witness to this truth.

When Elizabeth received a letter from John telling her he had "become dead" to his "former bustling actings in the world," she took the letter to the lord protector and begged again for her husband's release. Powerful though he was, Cromwell still feared the man who had once been a formidable enemy—a man now broken and physically ill from prison life, suffering from a wasting lung disease. He would not grant Elizabeth's plea.

By May 1656 John had become a convinced Quaker. He celebrated his conversion by writing *The Resurrection of John Lilburne now a Prisoner in Dover Castle*. The pamphlet was printed and widely circulated. It went into a second printing in less than a week. In it John made " a publike Declaration in print, of my real owning, and now living in . . . the life and power of those spirituallised people called Quakers."

The man who had fought through two and a half years of bloody civil war declared, in the pamphlet, "I am led up into power in Christ, by which I particularly can, and do hereby witness, that I am already dead, or crucified, to the very occasions, and real grounds of all outward wars, and carnal sword fightings and fleshy bustlings and contests; and that therefore I confidently now believe, I shall never hereafter be an user of a temporall sword more, nor a joyner with those that so do."

Although not given outright release from his Dover Castle prison, John was frequently allowed out on parole by mid-1656, sometimes for more than a day and as far away as Woolwich, Eltham, and other villages in Kent he may have known as a boy. When the birth of another child was expected in the summer of 1657, he took lodgings for Elizabeth and their children at Eltham. He was allowed to join them there but was scheduled to report back at his Dover Castle prison on August 29.

Shortly before he planned to leave Eltham, he became too weak to travel. Although he was only about forty-two years old, his body could no longer cope with the wasting lung disease and the effects of the many hardships he had suffered in and out of prison. On the day he was due back in Dover, he died, close to the woman he loved—the woman who loved him because of or in spite of the hardships they had undergone together in their seventeen years of bitter struggle for justice and human rights and liberties.

Cromwell lived only a year longer than Lilburne. By his final acts in the strange relationship between the two men, he showed unusual consideration toward Elizabeth and the three surviving children. He transferred to her the £2 weekly allowance John had received while in prison and arranged with Sir Arthur Haselrig for her to take possession of some more of the disputed County Durham lands. Cromwell's son and successor, Richard, continued the allowance. Under Richard's rule, the House of Commons action by which John had been fined £7000 was made void, and the Lilburne estate was relieved of a heavy financial burden.

John Lilburne's direct influence upon English politics ceased before the end of his life. Oliver Cromwell saw to that. Also, Cromwell made sure that the Leveller influence upon contemporary life would diminish. Lilburne's name occupies no large part in most English histories—he is not even mentioned in some. Yet the ideas he fought for with honesty and courage, even the words and phrases he wrote in his pamphlets, crop up again and again, without his name attached, in English and American political documents.

Religious liberty, a free press, free speech, separation of church and state, manhood suffrage, a government of law and not of men, equality of all persons before the law, an end to arbitrary imprisonment, an end to monopolies, the right of an accused person not to incriminate himself, the right of an accused person to see and study his indictment before a trial, the right of an accused person to be represented by counsel—all these ideas and more Lilburne believed in, eloquently wrote about, strenuously argued for, and helped to establish as recognized rights, as recognized truths. Some or all of them are included in the English Bill of Rights accepted by William and Mary in 1689, the Body of Liberties adopted by Massachusetts colonists in 1641, the Virginia Declaration of Rights, the American Declaration of Independence, the Constitution of the United States as originally adopted, the first ten amendments, or Bill of Rights, and the Constitution as it continues to grow.

Perhaps at his death John Lilburne left to future minds more than he, in the last years of his life, hoped for—more than most later generations have recognized as coming from him.

FOUR

George Mason

G eorge Mason of Gunston Hall was a man of contradictions and paradoxes. He never went to college, never to high school, or even to elementary school; yet he was one of the best-educated men of his time. He never was licensed to practice law, yet he was regarded in the English colonies of North America as one of the best authorities on constitutional law and the legal rights of individuals. Born in a rural colony, he was one of the founders of a nation—the United States of America.

The fourth George Mason to live in Virginia, he was the eldest son of the eldest son of the eldest son at a time when the eldest son had the right to inherit all the property of his deceased parents. Yet he believed that "all Men are born equally free and independent," and he worked for abolition of the law of primogeniture.

A descendant of English Royalists, a member of the Virginia aristocracy, a son of wealthy parents, a prosperous landlord and slaveowner, George Mason IV was an eloquent champion of the common man and a hater of the institution of slavery.

In 1651, two years after Charles I of England was beheaded, the great-grandfather of George Mason IV was living in Shakespeare country and loyally fighting for his king. He was at the battle of Worcester when Oliver Cromwell's forces routed Charles II and his Scottish allies. Shortly after the battle he decided that the wilderness of North America would be safer and pleasanter for Royalists than the placid fields and villages of England. He was prepared to become George Mason I of Virginia.

At that time Englishmen were being rewarded for persuading fellow Englishmen to emigrate to Virginia. The year after the battle of Worcester Great-grandfather George Mason, having persuaded several other persons to undertake the adventure of life in the new land, sailed the Atlantic, landed at Norfolk, and made his way up the Potomac River to the Northern Neck of Virginia. On rich tidewater land close to the river, a few miles south of Alexandria, he settled on the 900 acres he had earned, 50 acres for each of the 18 persons he had "caused to come into the colony."

About the same time other Royalist families were settling in Virginia. Among them were the ancestors of four early presidents of the United States: Washington, Jefferson, Madison, and Monroe.

George Mason I, II, and III fought American Indians.

Through merit or courtesy all of them acquired the military title colonel. George Mason IV did not fight Indians. His active military service, if any, must have been brief. A disease he referred to as "gout in my stomach," or simply "gout," sometimes complicated by painful "convulsive colic," plagued him most of his life. However, he seems to have inherited the colonel title along with hundreds of acres of land and scores of slaves.

He seems to have inherited, also, a surprising political liberalism. George Mason I had fought for his king and the established government when he lived in England. But in Virginia he supported the rebellion led by Nathaniel Bacon, a member of the House of Burgesses at the capital in Williamsburg; Bacon, an aristocrat and a large landholder, was trying to stop the exploitation of the small farmers by the wealthy of England and Virginia. George Mason II, at the time of the Glorious Revolution in England, 1688–89, was outspoken against the doctrines of King James II. George Mason III won fame as far away as Scotland for his opposition to a British navigation act he considered unjust.

BIRTH AND BOYHOOD

George Mason IV was born in 1725 on a large Virginia plantation situated where the Potomac River bends around Dogue's Neck, about fifteen miles downstream from Alexandria. His family owned land in Maryland as well as in Virginia. When George was five, his family moved from the plantation at Dogue's Neck to one in Maryland across the Potomac.

To supervise the work on his Virginia plantations George Mason III made frequent trips across the river. On one of those trips a sudden squall overturned his sailboat, and he was drowned. Surviving him were his widow, Ann Thomson Mason, and his children, George, ten years old; Mary, four; and Thomson, two.

In making his will, George Mason III may have been wiser than he knew. He had designated as guardians his wife and her relative by marriage, John Mercer, who lived downriver at Marlborough.

Ann Mason moved with the three children back to Virginia, occupied a house on the plantation named Chappawamsic, southwest of Dogue's Neck, and devoted her interests and energies to bringing up her small family. John Mercer, a lawyer, took over his legal duties as guardian and began his influence over the life and mind of George Mason IV.

At the age of eighteen Thomson Mason was sent to London to study law in the Middle Temple, as his grandfather Stevens Thomson and great-grandfather William Thomson had studied before him.

No record, no hint, exists that his older brother, George, ever attended college, not even at Willamsburg. No record exists that he attended an elementary or high school. He evidently received his early education at home. His mother's account books record that he was tutored from 1736 to 1739 by a Mr. Williams and in 1738 also by a Mr. Wylie, who received 845 pounds of tobacco for a year's services.

Most of George Mason's education that showed in later years came from the library of John Mercer at Marlborough. There George found not only a few hundred books on law but also a thousand or more books on general subjects by such authors as Milton, Pope, and Voltaire.

John Mercer had a quick temper, and the difficulties it brought him were George Mason's good fortune. Because of Mercer's insults to a county court, the Virginia House of

Burgesses pronounced him "forever disabled to practice as an attorney." The "forever" lasted for about ten years, years of critical importance to both Mercer and young George Mason.

During those ten years Mercer worked on an abridgement of the laws of Virginia. During much of that ten-year period, George Mason, of high school and college age, read in the Mercer library and worked closely with Mercer.

The Mercer abridgement included a comprehensive review of all British law and statutes recognized in Virginia, as well as acts of the colonial legislature. It was ultimately accepted by the House of Burgesses as the standard authority for county-court magistrates. More important, it helped to prepare George Mason IV to become the principal author of one of the most influential political documents of his time.

In 1746, when Mason turned twenty-one, he left his mother's home at Chappawamsic and went to live on one of the plantations he had inherited, the one at Dogue's Neck, overlooking the Potomac.

MARRIAGE AND LOCAL POLITICS

On the Dogue's Neck plantation in Virginia, George Mason was now farther from John Mercer's library than he had been in his mother's home, but he did not lose his appetite for reading or for the law.

He began to take an active part in the life of his community. He had developed an intense interest in the management of his plantation, growing tobacco, wheat, corn, and cotton, raising cattle and sheep, and cultivating fruit orchards.

At this time he renewed his interest in Ann Eilbeck of Mattawoman, an estate in Charles County, Maryland. The Eilbeck and the Mason families had been neighbors in Maryland. On April 4, 1750, Ann and George were married at Mattawoman. "She was somewhat taller than the middle size, & elegantly shaped," George wrote in the family Bible after Ann's death. "Her Eyes were black, tender & lively; her Features regular & delicate; her Complexion remarkably fair & fresh—Lilies and Roses (almost without a Metaphor) were blended there—and a certain inexpressible Air of Cheerfulness, Health, Innocence & Sensibility diffused over her Countenance form'd a Face the very Reverse of what is generally called masculine."

For his bride, Mason planned a new home, which was to be near his old home on the Virginia shore of the Potomac, on a peninsula now called Mason Neck. It was to be named for a Gunston Hall in Maryland that had been named for a Gunston Hall in England. Both the English and the Maryland Gunston halls had belonged in the Fowke family, maternal ancestors of Mason. The first Fowke in Virginia had left England at the time George Mason I had emigrated. The Gunston Hall of George Mason IV was completed in 1758 and still stands placidly overlooking the Potomac River.

Nine children were born to Ann and George. When Ann died of a slow fever in March 1773, the oldest was twenty years of age, the youngest three.

Mason's principal community interests were Fairfax County, the town of Alexandria, and Truro Parish. In 1754 Mason was appointed a trustee of Alexandria. Many of the trustees of Alexandria served also as unpaid gentlemen justices of the court of Fairfax County. Mason was one of the gentlemen justices. Another was his neighbor George Washington, who lived at Mount Vernon, about five miles upstream.

The court had charge of the county's administrative business, which included taxation and the condition of roads, bridges, and ferries. It also had charge of its judicial business, such as public prosecutions and cases between private parties. Failure to report taxable property was carefully watched for. On one occasion several prominent citizens, including George Mason and George Washington, were cited for having failed to report their fine carriages on their tax returns.

As a unit of the Church of England, the Truro Parish with its three or more churches had moral and charitable obligations that went beyond the religious needs and desires of its people. Covering a large area in northern Virginia, it had been created in 1732 by an act of the Virginia Assembly. At that time church and state were not separate.

George Mason was elected to the vestry of Truro Parish in 1749, the year before he was married. As a vestryman, he had contact with people of all classes and in many different situations.

The Truro vestry not only assessed the tithes upon parishioners. It collected and spent them. From year to year tithes varied from as low as twelve pounds of tobacco per head to as high as sixty pounds; usually it was about thirty pounds per head. A goodly part of the tithe money went for care of the unemployed or underemployed poor, especially the sick, the elderly, and orphans who had no kinfolk to care for them. By 1749 a beginning had been made toward organizing a health service; payments were made to doctors for caring for the ailing poor. In a year of great unemployment a special committee, of which Mason was a member, was named to prepare a plan for employing the able-bodied poor.

Children of the poor were apprenticed to various trades. The vestry named the trade and the wage for each child and, in addition, stipulated that the child was to be taught reading and writing.

Once every four years the vestry supervised the "processioning" or "beating of bounds" of all lands in the parish. The "beating of bounds" consisted of having men move in procession along the established boundary lines between all properties. In this way the vestry hoped to maintain the old lines and to keep the peace by preventing boundary disputes.

Mason was thirty-four years old before he served in his first public office above the local level; he was elected a delegate to the Virginia House of Burgesses in 1759. He had already begun to think of himself as ready for retirement.

Through his church and political offices in Fairfax County Mason had experienced ten years of knowing people as people and at close range—knowing the high, the low, and the in-between. He had served with Washington on the Fairfax County Court and on the Truro Parish vestry. In one election for vestrymen he had received the highest number of votes, Washington third highest.

John Mercer's library, the Fairfax County Court, the town of Alexandria, and the Truro Parish vestry—all were local elements in the political education of George Mason. Another element less local was the Ohio Company, chartered in 1748 to open for settlement the wilderness west of the Allegheny Mountains. For many years Mason was a stockholder and the treasurer of the Ohio Company. His experience with this company gave him a broad knowledge and a sympathetic understanding of the settlers and the native Americans of the western frontier and beyond.

THE FAIRFAX RESOLVES

Mason served in the House of Burgesses for less than a year. He was annoyed and impatient—especially in committee work—with what he considered the stupidity of human nature in the conduct of business in the House. More important to Mason than another term in the House of Burgesses were his family, his plantations, and Fairfax County. And "gout" made the journeys to Williamsburg difficult and painful.

Mason's influence, however, went far beyond Fairfax County. Gunston Hall was only a short distance off the main highway between Williamsburg and Philadelphia. Thomas Jefferson, James Madison, George Washington, and other colonial leaders were frequent visitors.

In 1765 the British Parliament, needing money to pay for the Seven Years War, passed the Stamp Act, which provided for a tax on publications and legal documents. Mason joined fellow colonials all up and down the Atlantic Coast in resistance to the act.

In the summer of 1766, after the Stamp Act had been repealed, a long letter by Mason was published in the *London Public Ledger*. Mason signed the letter "A Virginia Planter." He identified himself as a man "who spends most of his Time in Retirement, and has seldom medled in public Affairs, who enjoys a moderate but independent Fortune, and content with the Blessings of a private Station, equally disregards the Smiles & Frowns of the Great." He declared himself to be "an Englishman in his Principles, . . . firmly attached to the present royal Family upon the Throne, unalienably affected to his Majesty's sacred Person & Government, in the Defence of which he wou'd shed the last Drop of his Blood." He asserted that nine-tenths of the king's subjects in America were of the same sentiments. But, he declared, "Such another Experiment as the Stamp-Act wou'd produce a general Revolt in America."

Still needing money to pay for the Seven Years War, England in 1767 tried "such another Experiment as the Stamp-Act." It was the Townshend Act, by which a tax was levied on many things—glass, paper, printers' colors, tea. About three years later the tax was repealed on most of the items, but not on tea. And so the stage was set for the Boston Tea Party, which took place on December 16, 1773.

After the rowdy tea party about five hundred miles and seven or eight days to the northeast, the reluctant George Mason spent less time in retirement and he meddled in public affairs as never before. He and Washington led a drive in which 38 barrels of flour, 150 bushels of wheat, and £273 were pledged for "the industrious poor of the town of Boston." Then, with suggestions from Washington, Mason wrote the Fairfax Resolves, which were adopted "at a general Meeting of the Freeholders and Inhabitants of the County of Fairfax on Monday the 18th day of July 1774, at the Court House, George Washington Esquire Chairman."

The Fairfax Resolves traveled further in influence and effect than might usually be expected from action of the inhabitants of a single rural county. George Mason, who drafted them, had an unusual ability for putting political ideas into words. The Resolves were adopted with the support of George Washington, who was beginning to bulk large throughout the English colonies in North America. And they contained words, phrases, and ideas that had been politically powerful before and would be heard again.

> 1. RESOLVED that this Colony and Dominion of Virginia can not be considered as a conquered Country. . . . That our Ancestors, when they left their native Land, and setled in America, brought with them . . . the Civil-Constitution and Form of Government of the Country they came from; and were by the Laws of Nature and Nations, entitled to all it's Privileges, Immunities and Advantages; which have descended to us their Posterity and ought of Right to be as fully enjoyed, as if we had still continued within the Realm of England.

2. RESOLVED that the most important and valuable Part of the British Constitution, upon which it's very existence depends, is the fundamental Principle of the People's being governed by no Laws, to which they have not given their Consent, by Representatives freely chosed by themselves. . . .

Much more is in the twenty-four Fairfax Resolves. The idea of natural rights, or law of nature, which goes back at least as far as Stephen Langton, is in the fifth resolve: that "to extort from us our Money without our Consent . . . is totally incompatible with the Privileges of a free People, and the natural Rights of Mankind." In the sixth resolve is the statement "that Taxation and Representation are in their Nature inseparable."

In their historic meeting the inhabitants of Fairfax County resolved that trade with England ought to be cut off; that the growing of tobacco be stopped; that "Support and Assistance" be given to the town of Boston, which was suffering from "ministerial Vengeance"; that Virginians cordially join with their "Friends and Brethren of this and the other Colonies, in such Measures as shall be judged most effectual for procuring Redress of our Grievances." As for the slave trade: "We take this Opportunity of declaring our most earnest Wishes to see an entire Stop for ever to such a wicked cruel and unnatural Trade."

The men of Fairfax County declared in the twenty-third resolve their desire to continue dependence upon Great Britain. But they threatened independence. They beseeched the king "not to reduce his Subjects of America to a State of desperation, and to reflect, that from our Sovereign there can be but one Appeal." Washington, Mason, and the other Fairfax County resolvers knew that the king would know that the "one Appeal" was force of arms.

MORE RESOLVES

The Fairfax Resolves of July 18, 1774, soon traveled beyond the county of origin. In August, they were taken by Washington to an important meeting in Williamsburg. On October 20, nearly two years before the Declaration of Independence was adopted and signed, the Resolves formed the basis for proposals by the Continental Congress, in Philadelphia, to stop trade between the colonies and England.

For several months before the embattled farmers at Lexington and Concord "fired the shot heard round the world," colonists had been organizing themselves into volunteer military units and drilling with arms, and on June 15, 1775, the Continental Congress sought to create an army by appointing George Washington commander-in-chief of the combined colonial forces.

In July 1775 George Mason, at the insistence of his friends, including Washington, accepted public office as a member of the third Virginia Convention, which met in Richmond. Mason's health did not improve at the convention, which he regarded as "ill-conducted."

Even with Lexington, Concord, and Bunker Hill recently behind them, the delegates at the third Virginia Convention were not ready to declare for independence. Before the convention ended in August they announced, "We again, & for all, publickly and solemnly declare, before God & the world, that we do bear faith and allegiance to His Majesty George the Third, our only lawful & rightful King. . . ."

When the fourth Virginia Convention met in Williamsburg nine months later, sentiment had changed. Publication of Thomas Paine's *Common Sense* had given a push toward separation from the crown. On May 15, 1776, a month and a half before the Declaration of Independence was signed at Philadelphia, the convention delegates at Williamsburg

> RESOLVED unanimously, that the Delegates appointed to represent this Colony in General Congress be instructed to propose to that respectable body to declare the United Colonies free & independent states. . . .
>
> RESOLVED, unanimously, that a committee be appointed to prepare a DECLARATION OF RIGHTS & such a plan of Government as will be most likely to maintain peace & order in this Colony, & secure substantial & equal liberty to the people.

At home with "a smart fit of the Gout," George Mason was not in Williamsburg when the resolutions were passed, nor was he there for the rejoicing on the day after. On May 16, people turned out in large numbers. Soldiers paraded. The resolutions were read aloud. Toasts were given to "The American Independence States," to "The Grand Congress of the United States and their respective legislatures," and to "General Washington, and victory for the American arms." A burst of artillery and small-arms fire followed each toast.

A newspaper reported: "The *Union Flag* of the American states waved upon the Capitol during the whole of the Ceremony, which being ended, the soldiers partook of the refreshment provided for them, and the evening concluded with illuminations and other demonstrations of joy; every one seeming pleased that the domination of Great Britain was now at an end, so wickedly and tyrannically exercised for these twelve or thirteen years past, notwithstanding our repeated prayers and remonstrances for redress."

The second day after passage of the resolution recommending independence was a time for sober thinking in Williamsburg. The refreshments had been consumed. The rejoicing had ended. Delegates to the fourth convention had begun

to realize that declaring independence was not enough; it had
to be won.

Then, too, May 17 had been appointed by the Continental
Congress a day for "a General Fast throughout the United
Colonies." In Williamsburg, as part of the solemn occasion,
a religious service was held in one of the churches.

In the sober quiet of the fast day Mason arrived in Williamsburg. He was at once added to the committee that had
been appointed to draft the declaration of rights and the constitution or "plan of Government . . . most likely to maintain
peace & order" in Virginia and "secure substantial & equal
liberty to the people."

THE VIRGINIA DECLARATION OF RIGHTS

On the committee appointed to draft a declaration of
rights and a constitution for Virginia were thirty-three men in
addition to Mason. In the group were men of diverse backgrounds, opinions, and ways of living and thinking. The eastern
tidewater area was represented mainly by wealthy landowners who wore powdered wigs and copied the manners and
dress of London. The western part of the state was represented mainly by frontiersmen who lived in log cabins, wore
coonskin caps, and kept their long rifles handy.

George Mason, owner of Gunston Hall and long-time
shareholder in the Ohio Company, knew and understood the
men of both groups. He and Thomas Jefferson thought of the
powdered wig and the coonskin cap as equals. Both men had
the trust of both groups.

But how could a committee of thirty-four men, even if
they agreed politically, write a coherent declaration of rights
and a workable constitution?

"The Committee appointed to prepare a plan is, according to Custom, overcharged with useless Members," Mason wrote in a letter to his friend Richard Henry Lee at the Continental Congress in Philadelphia. "You know our Conventions. . . . We shall, in all probability, have a thousand ridiculous and impracticable proposals, & of course, a Plan form'd of hetrogenious, jarring & unintelligible Ingredients."

Mason was so well known for his skill as a writer of legal documents (and for his impatience in committee meetings) that the thirty-three other members of the committee willingly left to him the writing of the first draft of the Virginia Declaration of Rights and much of the constitution.

When Mason's first draft of the Declaration of Rights was submitted to the committee about a week later, four more rights were added. As all of these rights were in agreement with previous statements by Mason, they may have been added by him. The wording of Mason's draft was left almost intact.

With very few changes, the draft approved by the committee was accepted by the fourth Virginia Convention on June 12, 1776. Four of the paragraphs were combined into two.

The language of the first numbered paragraph gave the convention the most trouble. The committee report and Mason's draft declared that "all men are born equally free and independent, and have certain inherent natural rights. . . ."

Some slaveowners, fearing that "all men are born equally free" might give their slaves a claim to freedom, felt more comfortable with a revised wording: "That all men are (by nature) equally free and independent, and have certain inherent rights. . . ."

Largely because of the convictions and persistence of James Madison, Mason's paragraph on religion was amended. The final paragraph of the committee report had contained the statement "that all men should enjoy the fullest toleration in the exercise of religion." To Madison toleration was not enough; "the free exercise of religion" was required.

With a few exceptions the words in the Virginia Declaration of Rights were Mason's. Most of the ideas were his by adoption and assimilation. Many of the ideas were shared by other colonial leaders, but usually with less clarity and intensity. In origin the basic ideas were older than Mason, most of them older than any of the united colonies. Some of them had come from the authors of Magna Carta, some from the religious reformers and the Levellers of the seventeenth century—the inspirers or the authors of the English Bill of Rights of 1689. Some had come from John Locke and other recent English or French writers. All had undergone development in Mason's own mind during the thinking and the writing that went into the Fairfax Resolves, other public papers, and personal letters, and during conversations with Washington, Jefferson, Patrick Henry, and other colonial leaders.

Some of the ideas and words in the Virginia Declaration of Rights can be found in the Declaration of Independence. Some are in the original seven articles of the Constitution of the United States. Some are in the first ten amendments or Bill of Rights.

With justifiable pride Mason noted in a letter to an overseas correspondent in 1778 that the Virginia Declaration of Rights was "afterwards closely imitated by the other United States." Seven of the original thirteen states and Vermont adopted constitutions having separate bills of rights. Four others wrote into their constitutions provisions for the protection of certain rights.

Three drafts of the Virginia Declaration of Rights are known: the draft submitted by Mason to the committee appointed by the fourth Virginia Convention; the draft presented by the committee to the convention on May 27; the final draft, or a copy of the final draft, as accepted by the convention on June 12, 1776. Any one of the drafts merits side-by-side comparison with parts of the Declaration of Independence, with parts of the first seven articles of the Constitution, and with the Bill of Rights or first ten amendments to the Constitution. The final draft is printed at the end of this book.

Mason believed that all power is vested in the people. The magistrates—the elected or appointed government officials—are their trustees, their servants. The purpose of government is the happiness and safety and well-being of the people. If at any time the government fails in this purpose, the people—a majority of them—have the power and the right to replace that government with another. In becoming a member of society, man does not unconditionally surrender control over his natural rights: life, liberty, and use of property. He reserves the right to change society.

The first Virginia Assembly under the new constitution (Mason was one of the principal authors) met in the autumn of 1776. Surprisingly, Mason was a member, a delegate from Fairfax County. He continued to serve through most of the Revolutionary War, until the end of 1780.

He and his friends worked to pass laws that conformed to both the Virginia Declaration of Rights and the Virginia Constitution. Among the laws they favored were some that many members of the assembly considered too revolutionary: laws providing for general education, insuring religious liberty, ending slavery, abolishing primogeniture.

Of Mason at this time Jefferson wrote an appreciative description: "I had many occasional and strenuous coadjutors in debate, and one most steadfast, able and zealous, who was himself a host. This was George Mason, a man of the first order of wisdom among those who acted on the theatre of the Revolution, of expansive mind, profound judgment, cogent in argument, learned in the lore of our former constitution, and earnest for the republican change on democratic principles. His elocution was neither flowing nor smooth, but his language was strong, his manner most impressive, and strengthened by a dash of biting cynicism when provocation made it seasonable."

INDIANS AND THE NORTHWEST TERRITORIES

Unlike many of the colonists, George Mason believed that Indians, the native Americans, also had certain rights. Land should be bought from the native Americans and paid for, not taken by force or trickery. Treaties should be kept. Indian hunting grounds should not be invaded by white men with long rifles, killing the game on which the native people mainly depended for their living.

"Our people begun to settle upon the Indian hunting Grounds, yet full of Game," Mason wrote in 1792 to James Monroe, later president of the United States. "And to compleat the Business, the whole Indian Country, as far West as the Mississippi, and as far North as the Lake of the Woods, was laid off into separate States. . . . It is easy to conceive what Effect this wou'd have upon the Minds of the Indians. . . . It was shewing the Indians (to use a Phrase of their own) that we were preparing to drive them from the Face of the Earth; and it is no Wonder, that it has created a general Confederacy of the Indian Tribes against us."

In the same letter to Monroe, Mason wrote, "I hope when ever we treat again with the Indians, we shall be more moderate in our Demands."

Mason had bought tracts of land in Kentucky, then a

county of Virginia, and his long-time interest in the territory as far west as the Mississippi River had given him a good understanding of the causes of bloody conflict between the Indians and the whites.

At the time of his letter to Monroe attacks by Indians on frontier settlements had made war between the new nation and the Indian confederacy seem inevitable—almost a "necessity." But, Mason wrote, "I believe this Necessity is, in a great Measure, the Offspring of our own Misconduct."

During the Revolutionary War one of the vexing problems of the Continental Congress was caused by the western land claims of certain states. Virginia, Massachusetts, New York, and Connecticut held claims to large tracts of land in the area later known as the Northwest Territory, the land bordering the Great Lakes, north of the Ohio River. These tracts were justifiable causes of friction between the states with claims and the states without, and they caused disputes between states having adjoining claims.

For help in solving this seemingly unsolvable territorial problem Joseph Jones, a Virginia member of the Continental Congress, which was meeting tumultuously in Philadelphia, appealed in 1780 to George Mason, living peacefully in Virginia. Mason, though a member of his state assembly, planned to leave public life soon and lead a life of retirement at Gunston Hall.

To Jones's appeal Mason unexpectedly reacted as if it were an invitation to a battle for equal rights and justice. Stirred by "the importance of the subject," he brought together his extensive information about the western lands, his broad knowledge of law, and his unusual ability to put ideas on paper. In a letter of more than three thousand words addressed to Jones and dated July 27, 1780, Mason proposed a plan of settlement that outlasted the Continental Congress. Not only was most of the plan accepted by the Congress but seven years later it formed the basis of the Northwest Ordinance, which set the rules by which Ohio, Indiana, Illinois, Michigan, Wisconsin, and part of Minnesota were admitted to the Union. It helped to establish the principle of equal rights for states: that the rights of a state newly admitted to the Union were equal to the rights of any state previously admitted.

Repeatedly Mason spoke out in favor of this principle, most effectively at the Constitutional Convention in Philadelphia during the hot, humid summer of 1787. In a portion of his July 11 speech, as reported by James Madison, he stated, "Strong objections had been drawn from the danger to the Atlantic interests from new Western States. Ought we to sacrifice what we know to be right in itself, lest it should prove favorable to States which are not yet in existence? If the Western States are to be admitted into the Union as they arise, they must . . . be treated as equals, and subjected to no degrading discriminations. They will have the same pride & other passions which we have, and will either not unite with or will speedily revolt from the Union, if they are not in all respects placed on an equal footing with their brethren."

Settlement of the territorial problem of 1780, Mason knew, was being stalled by greed—greed for political power and greed for money.

Some of the powerful men in the thirteen original states looked upon the lands west across the mountains as threats to their political power. They did not want any part of those lands admitted to the Union with rights equal to the rights of their own states.

"Several gentlemen of great influence," Mason wrote in

his letter to Jones, had joined with some of the former American governors "and several of the British nobility and gentry in a purchase for a mere trifle, about the year 1773, from the Indians of a large tract of country, containing by their own computation between twenty and thirty millions of acres, on the northwest side the Ohio." Other men had formed a similar company and had bought a huge tract adjoining the other. "And if fame speaks truth," wrote Mason, "these two companies, since the declaration of American independence, have united their interests; which they have spared no ends to strengthen, by disposing of shares to members of Congress, &c."

Mason assured Jones that "the most judicious men" in the Virginia Assembly were "well disposed for the sake of cementing our union, and accelerating the completion of the confederation, to make great concessions to the United States."

Mason proposed ceding to the Union all of Virginia's vast territory north of the Ohio River; that is, all of Virginia except what is now Virginia, West Virginia, and the land called Kentucky, then a Virginia county. He was offering to the new nation more than fifty million acres—"ceding and relinquishing to the United States the right and title of Virginia, both in the soil and sovereignty of the country"—subject to certain conditions.

Mason's letter was intended not only for the eyes of Joseph Jones. It was intended also for the eyes and ears of other members of the Continental Congress, in particular those members representing states with western land claims.

"I trust," Mason wrote, "Virginia will be considered as acting upon a large and liberal scale, and sacrificing her own local interests to the general cause of America." Virginia's claim to liberality could be explained in part by the well-publicized exploits of Colonel George Rogers Clark.

[*125*]

MASON AND THE
NORTHWEST TERRITORIES

Early in the Revolutionary War the British, with the help of their Indian allies, took control of most of the western lands claimed by the eastern states. In the autumn of 1777, when the War for Independence was going badly, Clark rode into Williamsburg from his home across the mountains in Kentucky County. In his head, he had a bold plan for a campaign against the British in the western country—"the Illinois," he sometimes called it.

Governor Patrick Henry liked his plan. So did other influential Virginians, including Thomas Jefferson, George Wythe, and George Mason. In previous journeys to eastern Virginia, Clark had visited Mason and absorbed some of his ideas. A warm friendship between the brash young frontiersman and the staid elder statesman had developed. Each man admired the good qualities of the other.

When Clark rode back across the mountains, he carried with him a commission as colonel, the promise of financial backing from the state of Virginia, and the authority to raise and equip a small army to capture Kaskaskia and other British forts in the Illinois country.

Also he carried with him much advice from Mason. This advice was followed later by more advice conveyed in letters. Two adventurous years later Colonel Clark wrote Mason a report that was longer and more detailed than the official report he made to Governor Thomas Jefferson. In the report to Mason, written from the Falls of the Ohio (later Louisville) and dated November 19, 1779, Clark gave a graphic relation of his heroic campaign—the capture by his small army of the British forts at Kaskaskia, Cahokia, and Vincennes, and the wading of miles of icy floodwaters to recapture the fort at Vincennes after it had been lost to the British.

George Mason was a man of ideas rather than action, but he helped to make history through the influence of his character and his ideas on men of action. The first paragraph of Clark's long report to Mason began, "Continue to favour me with your valuable Lessons. Continue your Repremands as though I was your Son: when suspicious, think not that promotion or confer'd Honour will occation any unnecessary pride in me. You have infus'd too many of your Valuable precepts in me to be guilty of the like, or to shew any indifference to those that ought to be dear to me. It is with pleasure that I obey in transmiting to you a short sketch of my enterprise and proceeding in the Illinois as near as I can Recollect, or gather from memorandums."

In Philadelphia members of the Continental Congress, reading or listening to Mason's letter to Joseph Jones, were well aware of Clark's successful campaign and the fact that Virginia had sponsored and financed it. Clark's taking of western lands from the British had given Virginia a special claim—a sort of claim by conquest—to all western lands, including the tracts previously claimed by other states.

In Mason's letter to Jones, Virginia was taking the lead by liberally offering to cede, subject to certain conditions, her western lands to the Union. Other states with claims to western lands were conscience-bound to follow her example.

The first condition mentioned by Mason was that the territory ceded should be "laid out and formed into not less than two separate and distinct states or governments. The time and manner of doing it to be at the discretion of congress."

The second condition was that Virginia should be reimbursed by the United States for expenses of the Clark campaign. The third specified that French or Canadians in Kaskaskia and similar settlements who considered themselves Virginia citizens should have their land rights protected. Two conditions provided for grants of land to George Rogers Clark and the officers and men of his victorious army and another condition for grants of land to Virginia soldiers of the Continental Army.

The final condition provided, in part, that all land not granted to the soldiers and other persons mentioned above should be "considered as a common fund" for the benefit of present and future states. This condition would deny special privileges to the coastal states having land claims—states jealous of their political power. It also would deny to greedy land speculators the huge financial gains they had sought by purchasing land from the Indians "for a mere trifle."

Part of Mason's last condition read, "All purchases and deeds from any Indian or Indians, or from any Indian nation or nations, within any part of said territory, which have been or shall be made for the use or benefit of any private person or persons whatsoever shall be deemed and declared absolutely void and of no effect, in the same manner as if the said territory had still remained subject to, and part of the commonwealth of Virginia."

Otherwise, Mason argued, the most valuable part of the territory to be ceded by Virginia would be "applied to private purposes."

Mason's lengthy letter to Joseph Jones ended with one long and one very short sentence: "As I think I have some weight in our assembly, and more upon this than any other subject, I earnestly wish Congress may take up the consideration, and transmit reasonable proposals to our next session, that I may have an opportunity of giving them my aid; being anxious to do this last piece of service to the American Union, before I quit the Assembly, which I am determined to do at the end of the next session. I am, &c., G. M."

Mason did not wait till the end of the next session to quit the assembly, or House of Delegates. His attacks of "convulsive colic," or "gout" of his stomach, had become more severe, and he found himself increasingly at odds with other members of the assembly.

"I quitted my Seat in the House of Delegates, from a Conviction that I was no longer able to do any essential Service," he wrote in a long letter to a friend. "Some of the public Measures have been so contrary to my Notions of Policy and Justice, that I wished to be no further concern'd with, or answerable for them; and to spend the Remnant of my Life in Quiet & Retirement. Yet with all her Faults, my Country will ever have my warmest Wishes & Affections; and I wou'd at any Time, most cheerfully, sacrifice my own Ease & domestic Enjoyments to the Public Good."

Even though Mason was no longer a member of the assembly, he continued to have "weight" there. Most of the proposals in his letter to Jones, and many of his words, were in the assembly resolution of 1781 and the act of 1783 in which Virginia lands north and west of the Ohio River were ceded to the Union.

Living quietly at Gunston Hall, Mason did not relax his interest in public affairs. He corresponded frequently with Jefferson, with Virginia delegates to the Continental Congress, and with other friends of his still in office.

In late March 1779, at the end of a winter that had been dark for the Revolutionary cause, Mason received an especially gloomy letter. It was from his most distinguished neighbor, who was away from Mount Vernon heading a small army of discontented and discouraged men. General Washington wrote from camp that he had "beheld no day since the commencement of hostilities" in which he thought the liberties of the nation were "in such eminent danger as at present. . . . Indeed we seem to be verging so fast to destruction, that I am filled with sensations to which I have been a stranger till within these three months."

Toward the end of his letter, Washington asked Mason where our men of abilities are. "Why do they not come forth to save their Country? Let this voice my dear Sir call upon you— Jefferson & others."

Because of his "gout," Mason was always reluctant to hold public office. Perhaps his voluminous correspondence with Revolutionary leaders was one effective way of coming forth to save his country.

PRELUDE TO THE CONSTITUTION

On October 19, 1781, about two and a half years after Mason received his gloomy letter from Washington, Cornwallis surrendered at Yorktown to the writer of the letter. Not until September 3, 1783, almost two years later, did Great Britain formally acknowledge the independence of the United States. Almost four more years passed before delegates from twelve of the thirteen states met at Philadelphia, hoping "to form a more perfect Union."

The Revolutionary War had been fought by a loose confederation of thirteen states, each with sovereign rights that it guarded jealously. During the war Washington had become increasingly aware of the need for a strong central government. Thomas Paine, in one of his patriotic pamphlets, declared, "Our strength and happiness are continental, not provincial."

Efforts "to form a more perfect Union" were prompted not altogether by patriotism or even by politics. Mixed with idealism were the attitude of the army and economic self-interest.

Officers and men of the Continental Army had served for years without pay. They threatened not to disband until they had the money due them. Some Pennsylvania troops, vowing to collect their back pay from Congress, marched on Philadelphia. Congress quickly, although temporarily, moved to Princeton, New Jersey. The army wanted a strong central government. Only wise and prompt action by Washington prevented a military dictatorship.

Economic self-interest included paper money and its value (or lack of value), tariffs on goods transported from one state to another, and businesses of many kinds.

In 1782, when Noah Webster, later famous for his dictionaries, had a hard time copyrighting his famous *Elementary Spelling Book*, or "Blue-backed Speller," in thirteen states, he began agitating for copyright laws that would apply uniformly in all of them. He wrote pamphlets in favor of a centralized government, and he regarded his *Sketches on American Policy* (1785) as the first proposal for a federal constitution.

Another Webster, Pelatiah, a Philadelphia businessman, had argued shortly before for a federal constitution to replace the Articles of Confederation. Such a constitution would simplify business in the thirteen states. His *Dissertation of the Political Union and Constitution of the Thirteen United States of North America* (1783) was widely read. Pelatiah probably had a better right than Noah to be called the originator of the United States Constitution.

George Mason, George Washington, and other gentlemen of Virginia and Maryland owned stock in the Potomac

Company, founded to develop the Potomac River as "a channel of the extensive trade of a rising empire." Because several states, principally Virginia and Maryland, were involved, commerce on the river and plans for its future development were frequent causes of friction. Even the fish in the river were the cause of one dispute. Marylanders wanted the right to take fish on both shores of the Potomac.

In the hope of bringing economic and political peace between the two principal states, the Virginia Assembly appointed commissioners (one of them Mason) to consult with Maryland commissioners. On a blustery day in March 1785, at the invitation of Washington, the group met at Mount Vernon.

Mason had long distrusted the motives of men in power; power was so easily and so often abused. He feared what a strong central government or a strong chief executive would do to the rights of individuals. But the discussion at the Mount Vernon meeting and numerous private conversations with his neighbor Washington helped him to see clearly what he had already begun to see. The Articles of Confederation might win a war, but something more binding than the articles as they stood was needed to make a nation.

Mason "is renouncing his errors on the subject of the Confederation, and means to take an active part in the amendment of it," Madison wrote to Jefferson on April 23, 1787. The owner of Gunston Hall had decided that, even though he continued to suffer from the "gout," a time had come for him to sacrifice his "own Ease & domestic Enjoyments to the Public Good."

In the spring of 1786, at the insistence of Washington, Mason had become a candidate for election as one of the two delegates to represent Fairfax County in the Virginia Assembly. He had been elected. The following spring he was named one of the seven delegates to represent Virginia in the Federal Constitutional Convention at Philadelphia.

For the first time since his retirement from the Virginia Assembly in 1780 Mason was officially serving his state. For six years he had refused requests and pleas of his friends to be named or elected to public office.

As Mason set out for Philadelphia in early May 1787 this man of sixty-two who hated to be away from Gunston Hall was starting the longest journey of his life. This man who hated committee meetings and conventions of any kind was on his way to attend one of the most complicated conventions of all time. This man who distrusted a strong central government was traveling with the expectation that he would eventually approve a strengthening of the present government—how much he would decide at the convention.

As he traveled he thought not only of duties ahead but of his family and friends back home. Though he had become recognized and valued as a statesman, he was still basically a Virginia plantation owner and family man. At Baltimore he wrote to his sons William and Thomson at Gunston Hall, giving them advice about their business affairs. A year and a half later Thomson would move with his family to his own plantation, Hollin Hall, a gift from his father; the land adjoined Washington's Mount Vernon estate. Later William would move to Mattawoman, the old Eilbeck plantation in Maryland, a gift from his father. Mason's daughters were married and lived on plantations their father had given them, most of them near Gunston Hall.

Shortly after arriving in Philadelphia, Mason wrote to his second wife, Sarah Brent, whom he had married in 1780. Also, he wrote to his eldest son, George, who lived on the nearby plantation his father had given him—Lexington, named for the first battle of the Revolutionary War.

Not all of the delegates, or deputies, had arrived in Philadelphia, Mason wrote in his letter to George. The convention had not yet been convened. The Virginia delegates, all of them present, met for two or three hours every day "in order to form a proper Correspondence of Sentiments." They were working on a formula, eventually known as the Virginia Plan, for reorganizing the government. It would be presented to the convention as a replacement for the Articles of Confederation.

Mason was convinced of the importance of the convention and anticipated its problems.

"The Expectations & Hopes of all the Union center in this Convention," he wrote his son George. "God grant that we may be able to concert effectual Means of preserving our Country from the Evils which threaten us."

The plan of government favored by the Virginians consisted of a great national council (two legislative branches), an executive, and a judiciary system.

About this plan Mason expressed both misgivings and hope: "It is easy to foresee that there will be much Difficulty in organizing a Government upon this great Scale, & at the same time reserving to the State Legislatures a sufficient Portion of Power for promoting & securing the Prosperity & Happiness of their respective Citizens. Yet, with a proper Degree of Coolness, Liberality & Candour (very rare Commodities by the Bye) I doubt not but it may be effected."

In his letter Mason mentioned the presence of deputy George Washington, who was to preside at the convention.

Of personal matters he wrote, "We found travelling very expensive, from eight to nine Dollars Per Day. In this City the Living is cheap. We are at the old Indian Queen in 4th.

Street, where we are very well accommodated, & have a good Room to ourselves. . . . Doctr. Franklin enquired very particularly & kindly after you, as did also his Grandson. Remember me kindly to Betsy [young George's wife], my little Pett, to the Family at Gunston Hall, to Mr. Massey, Mr. Cockburn and our other Friends. I am, dear George, Your Affecte. Father, G. Mason."

For city life Mason had little liking or patience. He had more interest in prospects for the crops of wheat and tobacco at home.

"I begin to grow heartily tired of the etiquette and nonsense so fashionable in this city," he wrote son George after being in Philadelphia little more than a week. "It would take me some months to make myself master of them, and that it should require months to learn what is not worth remembering as many minutes, is to me so discouraging a circumstance as determines me to give myself no manner of trouble about them."

MAKING THE CONSTITUTION— THE FORM OF GOVERNMENT

By May 25 seven states were represented by delegates, and the Federal Constitutional Convention opened for official business with the election of Washington as its presiding officer.

After the real work of the convention began on May 29 with the introduction of the Virginia Plan, Mason had little time for Philadelphia's "etiquette and nonsense." In the debates that followed, he was one of the delegates who addressed the house most often. Others were fellow Virginian James Madison, later to be president of the United States, Roger Sherman of Connecticut, Elbridge Gerry of Massachusetts, and James Wilson and Gouverneur Morris of Pennsylvania.

The basic problems before Mason and other members of

the Constitutional Convention of 1787 were not like those faced by rebels in twelfth- or seventeenth-century England. Stephen Langton and the rebellious nobles of the twelfth century were trying to reform a government that already existed. They were willing even to accept the monarch they had rebelled against if he would become less tyrannical and restore their ancient rights. John Lilburne and most other English rebels of the seventeenth century were trying to regain the precious individual rights they had lost, and gain a few more. They had little interest in making a new form of government. A monarchy or a commonwealth was good enough for them. They did not foresee that one of the rebels, as lord protector, would become a tyrant.

At Philadelphia in the eighteenth century were gathered representatives of sovereign states that recently had violently asserted their sovereignty. The states were no longer part of a monarchy. Each was a separate entity that for about a decade had been bound to twelve other entities in a "league of friendship" by the Articles of Confederation and a war against a common enemy. What, if anything, should continue to hold these entities together? Their representatives had considerable freedom to choose any form of government that to them seemed suitable.

On the day after introduction of the Virginia Plan, the delegates decided not to try merely to amend the Articles of Confederation. They voted to establish a national government "consisting of a supreme Legislative Executive & Judiciary."

In the debate that preceded the vote Mason had criticized "the present confederation" and stated that "such a Govt. was necessary as could directly operate on individuals, and would punish those only whose guilt required it." He pointed out that "punishment could not in the nature of things be executed on the States collectively."

The Constitution establishing the national government was not to be a treaty between states but the supreme law of the land, the delegates decided. But what or who should form the base of the government—the states or the people?

The delegates to the convention were not only the representatives of states, men reluctant to surrender the power and privileges of their states; they were also men of property—lawyers, merchants, farmers, country gentlemen, educators, politicians. They were not the common people or the common soldiers who had fought the Revolutionary War. In their deliberations they seemed to have more interest, more faith, in property than in "the people."

Many of them wanted their national legislature to be elected by their state legislatures (also composed of men of property) rather than by the people themselves. Many of the delegates seemed close to forgetting the Declaration of Independence and its brave words—"all Men are created equal."

Like the other delegates, Mason was a man of property—in fact, of more property than most of the others. Perhaps through idealism, perhaps through perversity, he kept reminding the other delegates of his faith in the people. He spoke of "the Genius of the People." He referred to "the people of America . . . so jealous of their liberties." More than any other delegate he kept before the convention the rights of the people. Throughout the deliberations he seemed almost to be speaking and voting against himself and his best interests.

The Virginia Plan provided for two branches of the national legislature. Members of the first or larger branch of the legislature should be elected by the people of the several states. When this provision was presented to the convention by Governor Edmund Randolph of Virginia, Sherman of Connecticut opposed it. Election should be by state legislatures, he said. The people "should have as little to do as may be about the Government." They lack information "and are constantly liable to be misled."

Elbridge Gerry of Massachusetts agreed with Sherman. The people, he said, "are the dupes of pretended patriots."

Mason's reply to Sherman and Gerry on May 31, 1787, was reported by James Madison, a Virginia delegate, who kept a comprehensive record of the convention proceedings:

> MR. MASON, argued strongly for an election of the larger branch by the people. It was to be the grand depository of the democratic principle of the Govt. It was, so to speak, to be our House of Commons—It ought to know & sympathise with every part of the community; and ought therefore to be taken not only from different parts of the whole republic, but also from different districts of the larger members of it, which had in several instances particularly in Virga., different interests and views arising from difference of produce, or habits &c &c. He admitted that we had been too democratic but was afraid we sd. incautiously run into the opposite extreme. We ought to attend the rights of every class of the people. He had often wondered at the indifference of the superior classes of society to this dictate of humanity & policy; considering that however affluent their circumstances, or elevated their situations, might be, the course of a few years, not only might but certainly would, distribute their posterity throughout the lowest classes of Society. Every selfish motive therefore, every family attachment, ought to recommend such a system of policy as would provide no less carefully for the rights and happiness of the lowest than of the highest orders of Citizens.

James Wilson of Pennsylvania and Madison joined Mason in arguing that members of the larger branch of the legislature should be elected by the people. Madison said that he considered "the popular election of one branch of the national legislature as essential to every plan of free Government." Two other delegates spoke against popular election.

Should members of the first, or larger, branch of the

national legislature be elected directly by the people? The vote by states, as reported by Madison: Massachusetts, New York, Pennsylvania, Virginia, North Carolina, and Georgia, ay; New Jersey and South Carolina, no; the Connecticut and Delaware delegations were divided. New Hampshire delegates were not yet present. Rhode Island voters had not been able to agree long enough to elect delegates and were never represented at the convention. Madison did not report a vote by Maryland delegates.

Three weeks later the question was reconsidered. Again Mason argued for popular election. "It is the only security for the rights of the people," he said.

The vote as reported by Madison: nine states, ay; one state, no; one state delegation divided.

An important victory for the people's rights had been won. The people themselves would elect members of the larger branch of the national legislature, soon to be known as the House of Representatives.

Mason argued persistently that all money bills should have their origin in the House of Representatives, with its members elected directly by the people.

If members of the second, or smaller, branch, the Senate, not elected directly by the people, should "have the power of giving away the people's money," he said on July 6, "they might soon forget the source from whence they received it. We might soon have an aristocracy."

When qualifications of voters were considered by the delegates, Mason again stood for the rights of the common people. Morris of Pennsylvania had moved to amend an article of the proposed Constitution so that the right of suffrage would be restricted to freeholders, men who owned land or other property.

"Give the votes to people who have no property," said

Morris, "and they will sell them to the rich who will be able to buy them."

Freeholders were the best guardians of liberty, declared John Dickinson of Delaware, and only they should have the right to vote.

A few other delegates argued in favor of limiting the suffrage to freeholders. But Mason, Madison, Benjamin Franklin, and others spoke eloquently against limitation. In Mason's opinion, "Every man having evidence of attachment to & permanent common interest with the Society ought to share in all its rights & privileges."

The vote on the motion to limit the vote to freeholders (landowners or other men of property), as reported by Madison: 1 state, ay; 7 states, no; 1 state, divided; 1, not present. Another victory for the common people!

Mason argued very persuasively for some measures he favored, not persuasively enough for others.

During the discussions on the executive or president, he argued for a seven-year term without eligibility for a second term. A single-term limitation would remove from the executive the temptation to intrigue for an additional term.

He opposed giving the power of war to the executive, "because [he was] not safely to be trusted with it"; or to the Senate, "because [it was] not so constructed as to be entitled to it." He was "for clogging rather than facilitating war." He was for facilitating peace.

He tried, and failed, to get inserted into the Constitution a phrase intended to secure "the liberties of the people . . . against the danger of standing armies in time of peace."

He argued that the executive should be impeachable while in office. "Shall any man be above Justice?" he asked. "Above all shall that man be above it, who can commit the most extensive injustice?" He favored punishing both the principal offender and his accomplices.

He asked why causes of impeachment should be limited to treason and bribery. "Treason as defined in the Constitution will not reach many great and dangerous offences." He suggested adding "maladministration." Later, according to Madison's report, Mason substituted "other high crimes & misdemesnors agst. the State." The House of Representatives accepted Mason's substitute wording, eight states to three, Madison reported.

Mason believed that the president should not have the power to pardon acts of treason.

He proposed the establishment of an executive council of six members to advise the president. The members would be appointed by the House or by the Senate. Benjamin Franklin seconded the motion. Wilson, Dickinson, and Madison spoke in favor of it. Franklin said he thought that "a Council would not only be a check on a bad President but a relief to a good one."

The motion was lost. A motion authorizing the president to call for written opinions of the heads of departments was carried.

Mason believed in and argued for separation of the three branches of government. "The purse & the sword ought never to get into the same hands, whether Legislative or Executive."

The office of the vice-president, Mason declared, was "an encroachment on the rights of the Senate; . . . it mixed too much the Legislative & the Executive, which as well as the Judiciary departments ought to be kept as separate as possible."

"Afraid of monopolies of every sort," Mason did not think they were authorized by the Constitution.

Alert for possible causes of corruption, he advocated that a member of the legislature, while in office, could hold no other government position. Unlike most of his colleagues, he opposed giving the president, with approval of the Senate, the power to appoint judges of the Supreme Court. Such power might give the president "an influence over the Judiciary department itself."

MAKING THE CONSTITUTION— SLAVERY AND NAVIGATION, THE BIG BARGAIN

Although Mason owned about one hundred slaves, he regarded slavery as morally wrong. It was harmful to the slaveowner as well as the slaves. He believed that in the new nation all slaves should be freed as soon as practicable. They should first be educated so that they would know how to make good use of their freedom. Because slaves had long been regarded as property, Mason believed that at the time of emancipation slaveowners should be paid for their freed slaves.

Emancipation might be several years in the future, Mason thought. But he insisted that the importation of slaves, the slave trade, "diabolical in itself, and disgraceful to mankind," should be ended by the Constitution.

On August 6, Article VII, Section 4, of the Constitution read as follows: "No tax or duty shall be laid by the Legislature on articles exported from any State; nor on the migration or importation of such persons as the several States shall think proper to admit; nor shall such migration or importation be prohibited."

No mention of slaves or slavery or the slave trade here! Only two innocent-looking words—*such persons*. In plain words, the slave trade was to be legalized.

[*142*]

How could men who subscribed to the sentiments in the Declaration of Independence baldly use the word "slave" in the Constitution that was intended to guarantee their own freedom?

On August 21 discussion of Section 4 of Article VII was begun. Luther Martin of Maryland proposed to amend the section to allow a prohibition or a tax on the importation of slaves. He considered the importation of slaves unreasonable; "it was inconsistent with the principles of the revolution and dishonorable to the American character to have such a feature in the Constitution." Three delegates spoke in favor of the section as it was, and the House adjourned for the day.

At the start of the session the following day Sherman of Connecticut announced that, though he disapproved of the slave trade, he was for leaving Section 4 as it stood. He urged on the convention "the necessity of despatching its business."

Mason promptly responded with one of the most impassioned speeches of the Constitutional Convention. Some things, he evidently believed, were more important to the convention than "despatching its business." Putting an end to the slave trade was one of them. The full text of Mason's speech has not been preserved—only Madison's report:

> COL. MASON. This infernal trafic originated in the avarice of British Merchants. The British Govt. constantly checked the attempts of Virginia to put a stop to it. The present question concerns not the importing States alone but the whole Union. The evil of having slaves was experienced during the late war. Had slaves been treated as they might have been by the Enemy, they would have proved dangerous instruments in their hands. But their folly dealt by the slaves, as it did by the Tories. He mentioned the dangerous insurrections of the slaves in Greece and Sicily; and the instructions given by Cromwell to the Commissioners sent to Virginia, to arm the servants & slaves, in case other means of

obtaining its submission should fail. Maryland & Virginia he said had already prohibited the importation of slaves expressly. N. Carolina had done the same in substance. All this would be in vain if S. Carolina & Georgia be at liberty to import. The Western people are already calling out for slaves for their new lands, and will fill that Country with slaves if they can be got thro' S. Carolina & Georgia. Slavery discourages arts & manufactures. The poor despise labor when performed by slaves. They prevent the immigration of Whites, who really enrich & strengthen a Country. They produce the most pernicious effect on manners. Every master of slaves is born a petty tyrant. They bring the judgment of heaven on a Country. As nations can not be rewarded or punished in the next world they must be in this. By an inevitable chain of causes & effects providence punishes national sins, by national calamities. He lamented that some of our Eastern brethren had from a lust of gain embarked in this nefarious traffic. As to the States being in possession of the Right to import, this was the case with many other rights, now to be properly given up. He held it essential in every point of view that the Genl. Govt. should have power to prevent the increase of slavery.

Sharp argument for and against Section 4 of Article VII followed Mason's bitter condemnation of slavery. It was ended temporarily when the delegates agreed to a suggestion by Morris of Pennsylvania that three subjects, the slave trade, taxes on imports, and navigation, be referred to a committee. "These things may form a bargain among the Northern & Southern States," Morris said.

A bargain was formed in the Committee of Eleven to which the suggestion by Morris was referred on August 22. The committee reported on Friday, August 24.

The last part of Section 4 of Article VII had been revised: "The migration or importation of such persons as the several States now existing shall think proper to admit, shall not be prohibited by the Legislature prior to the year 1800, but a tax or duty may be imposed on such migration or importation at a rate not exceeding the average of the duties laid on imports."

Still no mention of slaves or the slave trade—only "such persons" and "such migration or importation."

To be stricken out was Section 6 of Article VII: "No navigation act shall be passed without the assent of two thirds of the members present in each House."

The proposed revision of Section 4 would permit the slave trade, demanded by some southern states, to continue for at least thirteen more years. The proposed elimination of Section 6 would permit passage of navigation acts by a simple majority (instead of a two-thirds majority). These acts were favorable to northern states, which depended heavily on shipping.

Debate on the bargain did not end on Friday, August 24. It continued on Saturday, August 25, and several hot days thereafter.

Charles Pinckney of South Carolina moved to strike out 1800 as the date limiting the importation of slaves and insert the year 1808.

The motion was seconded by Nathaniel Gorham of Massachusetts, who opposed slavery but was willing to compromise himself as well as the issue.

Madison objected to the motion: "Twenty years will produce all the mischief that can be apprehended from the liberty to import slaves. So long a term will be more dishonorable to the National character than to say nothing about it in the Constitution."

Voting ay on the motion, Madison reported, were New Hampshire, Massachusetts, Connecticut, Maryland, North Carolina, South Carolina, Georgia. Voting no: New Jersey, Pennsylvania, Delaware, Virginia.

Northern states were willing to extend the importation of slaves for twenty more years in exchange for a promise of greater ease in passing navigation acts favorable to them. Slave trade in exchange for shipping!

The duty on imported slaves was discussed.

"Not to tax," commented Mason, "will be equivalent to a bounty on the importation of slaves."

Madison declared it "wrong to admit in the Constitution the idea that there could be property in men."

Agreed to and added to the twenty-year extension of slave importation was the clause, "But a tax or duty may be imposed on such importation not to exceed ten dollars per person."

The slave trade side of the bargain was finally written into the Constitution as Article I, Section 9, Paragraph one and is still there for all the world to see.

The navigation side of the bargain was covered in part by eliminating Section 6 of Article VII and in part by accepting provisions that got into the Constitution as Article I, Section 9, Paragraph six: "No preference shall be given by any regulation of commerce or revenue to the ports of one State over those of another; nor shall vessels bound to, or from, one State, be obliged to enter, clear, or pay duties in another."

MAKING THE CONSTITUTION—THE END

A preamble for the Constitution did not appear in reported deliberations of the convention at Philadelphia until Monday, August 6, 1787.

Some delegates had favored keeping the states as sovereign units: "We, the states. . . ." At its first appearance the Preamble began, "We the people of the States of New Hampshire, Massachusetts, Rhode-Island and Providence Plantations" (plus ten other states named), and ended, "do ordain, declare, and establish the following Constitution for the Government of Ourselves and our Posterity." Here the people were included not as individuals but as residents of the states.

As the Preamble was presented to the convention on Wednesday, September 12, by the Committee on Style and Arrangement and, except for insignificant changes, as it was finally accepted, it read, "We, the people of the United States, in order to form a more perfect Union, establish justice, insure domestic tranquility, provide for the common defense, promote the general welfare, and secure the blessings of liberty to ourselves and our posterity, do ordain and establish this Constitution for the United States of America."

"We, the people," not "We, the States," not "We, the people of the States of . . . ," not "We, the President of the United States," not "We, the Secretary of State," but "We, the people of the United States," living, breathing individuals who made the United States what it was and would make it what it is.

For four months the convention delegates had been hearing Mason's references to "the people" ringing in their ears. They may even have remembered some of the words and the meaning of the Declaration of Independence.

After the wording and arrangement of the Constitution had been agreed to, Mason proposed, almost shyly, that the principles of individual rights for which he had spoken and written most of his adult life should be included.

From Madison's report for September 12: "He [Mason] wished the plan [Constitution] had been prefaced with a Bill of Rights, & would second a Motion if made for the purpose. It would give great quiet to the people; and with the aid of State declarations, a bill might be prepared in a few hours."

Gerry of Massachusetts moved for a committee to prepare a bill of rights. Mason seconded the motion.

Sherman of Connecticut remarked that he was for securing the rights of the people, but that many states already had bills of rights which were sufficient.

Mason reminded him, "The Laws of the U.S. are to be paramount to State Bills of Rights." Ten states voted against Gerry's motion. The Massachusetts delegation was recorded as absent. No victory for individual rights or the common people here!

On July 23 Mason had argued at length for submitting the Constitution to the people instead of to the state legislatures for ratification—"to the people with whom all power remains that has not been given up in the Constitutions derived from them." He had stated that "this doctrine should be cherished as the basis of free Government."

Nearly two hot, humid months later he was of the same mind. On September 15, another Saturday, he spoke in support of a suggestion by Edmund Randolph, governor of Virginia, that the Constitution be submitted to state conventions; any amendments offered by the state conventions "should be submitted to and finally decided on by another general Convention."

Mason contended that the Constitution had been formed "without the knowledge or idea of the people."

"A second Convention," he reasoned, "will know more of the sense of the people, and be able to provide a system more consonant to it." He said it was "improper to say to the people, take this or nothing." As the Constitution then stood, he could not give it his support or his vote in Virginia; and he could not sign at the convention what he could not support in his state. "With the expedient of another Convention," as proposed by Governor Randolph, he could sign.

The final lines of Madison's report for Saturday, September 15, read as follows:

"On the question on the proposition of Mr. Randolph. All the States answered—no.

"On the question to agree to the Constitution, as amended. All the States ay.

"The Constitution was then ordered to be engrossed.

"And the House adjourned."

Two days later, Monday, September 17, 1787, in the twelfth year of independence of the United States of America, the engrossed Constitution—without a bill of rights—was read to the assembled delegates.

Delegate Benjamin Franklin, aged and infirm, had prepared a speech, which was read for him by fellow Pennsylvanian James Wilson. A microsummary of Franklin's sentiments: "I agree to this Constitution with all its faults." Other speakers announced that they would sign the document, but some had reservations about it.

Governor Randolph sadly, apologetically, announced that he could not sign. He said he was taking a step that might be the most awful of his life, but it was one dictated by his conscience.

Gerry described the painful feelings of his situation and announced that he would not sign.

Martin had left Philadelphia in disgust several days before.

Mason did not speak on the seventeenth, Madison's report indicates. He had already announced his intention not to sign. Later he wrote out in detail his objections to the Constitution and had several copies made. One copy of these objections he sent to his old friend George Washington. Once thereafter Washington referred to Mason as "my neighbor and *quondam* friend."

Mason's written objections to the Constitution had cooled the cordial feelings of the master of Mount Vernon toward his neighbor at Gunston Hall.

MASON'S OBJECTIONS TO
THE CONSTITUTION

Paradoxically, the Constitution of the United States of America, as done in convention, September 17, 1787—the document that was to guarantee the liberties the Declaration of Independence had proclaimed and for which the Revolutionary War had been fought—contained no reference to freedom of speech, press, or religion. It contained no mention of the people's right to assemble peaceably or to petition the government for redress of grievances, no mention of the people's right to be secure against unreasonable searches and seizures. It contained no mention of the quartering of troops on civilian populations. It contained no promise of speedy and public trial by jury, with the right of the accused to be informed of the nature of the accusation against him; no mention of the right of the accused to examine witnesses against him or to call witnesses in his defense. It made no mention of cruel and unusual punishment. Yet the president it had created possessed more power than the king of England.

Mason's objections to the Constitution that he and three other delegates refused to sign are worthy of study. The most serious faults Mason cited were corrected in 1791 by the first ten amendments, or Bill of Rights, a direct descendant from the Virginia Declaration of Rights, written by Mason.

Some other faults have been corrected in the years since then. What improvements in the federal government could be made by responding affirmatively to more of Mason's objections?

[*150*]

Here are a few of the objections Mason made to the Constitution as he wrote them about September 16, 1787, on blank pages of one of the copies printed for convention delegates:

There is no Declaration of Rights, and the laws of the general government being paramount to the laws and constitution of the several States, the Declarations of Rights in the separate States are no security. Nor are the people secured even in the enjoyment of the benefit of the common law.

The Judiciary of the United States is so constructed and extended, as to absorb and destroy the judiciaries of the several States; thereby rendering law as tedious, intricate and expensive, and justice as unattainable, by a great part of the community, as in England, and enabling the rich to oppress and ruin the poor.

The President of the United States has the unrestrained power of granting pardons for treason, which may be sometimes exercised to screen from punishment those whom he had secretly instigated to commit the crime, and thereby prevent a discovery of his own guilt.

Under their own construction of the general clause, at the end of the enumerated powers, the Congress may grant monopolies in trade and commerce, constitute new crimes, inflict unusual and severe punishments, and extend their powers as far as they shall think proper; so that the State legislatures have no security for the powers now presumed to remain to them, or the people for their rights.

There is no declaration of any kind, for preserving the liberty of the press, or the trial by jury in civil causes; nor against the danger of standing armies in time of peace.

Among the other objections Mason enumerated in his bold handwriting were the extension of the slave trade, which, he wrote, would "render the United States weaker, more vulnerable, and less capable of defence," and "that unnecessary officer the Vice-President, who for want of other employment is made president of the Senate, thereby dangerously blending the executive and legislative powers, besides always giving to some one of the States an unnecessary and unjust pre-eminence over the others."

BACK HOME IN VIRGINIA

On his return to Virginia from the Constitutional Convention in Philadelphia Mason was not a hero. The people of Fairfax County were strongly in favor of ratifying the Constitution. When Mason spoke in public against ratification, crowds were unfriendly. Some hearers heckled him. Legend records one of his exchanges with a heckler.

"Mr. Mason," a heckler called out, "you are an old man, and the public notices that you are losing your faculties."

"Sir," Mason snapped, "the public will never notice when you lose yours."

A Richmond newspaper criticized Mason and his prominent friend Richard Henry Lee for the "barefaced impudence and folly" of their public protests. "As for Mr. Mason, poor old man, he appears to have worn his judgment entirely threadbare and ragged in the service of his country."

At the Virginia ratifying convention in Richmond, in 1788, Mason joined the patriot orator Patrick Henry in opposing ratification. He repeated many of the objections he had made in Philadelphia. He continued to fear and warn against the power of the general government over the states and the people. He especially feared the power given the general government to tax the people directly. In a country as large and diverse as the United States officials of the general government could not truly represent the people. Officials having the power to tax, if true representatives, "ought to mix with the people, think as they think, feel as they feel, ought to be perfectly amenable to them, and thoroughly acquainted with their interest and condition."

On June 25, 1788, after about three weeks of debate, the Virginia ratifying convention voted by a small majority to accept the federal Constitution. Two days after the ratification vote, the Committee on Amendments presented a report containing a bill of rights that closely followed in substance and wording much of Mason's 1776 Virginia Declaration of Rights. The report was accepted and later was given to Virginia representatives to be taken to New York in 1789 and recommended "to the consideration" of the first session of the first national Congress as amendments to the Constitution.

Somewhat embittered by his experiences in Philadelphia and Richmond, Mason retired to Gunston Hall. But he closely followed the progress of the proposed amendments—*his* amendments—to the Constitution as they were being debated by the Congress and ratified by the states. To him, and also to Jefferson, the amendment finally accepted as the tenth was the most important: "The powers not delegated to the United States by the Constitution, nor prohibited by it to the States, are reserved to the States respectively, or to the people."

George Mason hoped that this amendment and the other nine which together became known as the Bill of Rights, would secure to the states and the people the rights that a too powerful central government would destroy, the truths that the Declaration of Independence had proclaimed.

"I have received much Satisfaction from the Amendments to the federal Constitution, which have lately passed the House of Representatives; I hope they will also pass the Senate," Mason wrote to a friend in September 1789. "With two or three further Amendments . . . I cou'd chearfully put my Hand and Heart to the new Government."

Adoption of the first ten amendments with their safe-guards for states' rights and individual liberties helped to soften Mason's attitude toward the Constitution.

When one of Virginia's first two senators died in 1790, Mason was appointed to replace him. But the master of Gunston Hall declined the appointment. His ill health was by this time keeping him confined to his house—even to his room—for long periods.

His sons and daughters, their families, and the Gunston Hall farm crops were his chief interests, but he continued to follow national and even international affairs. At the beginning of the French Revolution he wrote to his son John in France, "I heartily wish the french Nation Success in establishing their new Government, upon the Principles of Liberty, & the sacred Rights of human Nature; but I dread the Consequences of their Affairs remaining so long in an unsetled State."

To the end of his life Mason had the respect of the great Americans of his time. Though he was several years older than Jefferson, the two men thought alike and were active collabora-tors and correspondents for a score of years. Their lively friendship continued longer than that.

George Mason of Gunston Hall died in the afternoon of Sunday, October 7, 1792, at the age of sixty-seven. Exactly a week before, he and Jefferson had held a lengthy conversation.

Jefferson was on his way from Monticello to Philadelphia, where Congress was to meet in November. He had stopped at Mount Vernon to see Washington before he turned in at the road to Gunston Hall. Soon he was to become the leader of the party that sought to carry out the ideals held by George Mason, protecting the rights of the states and the people against an all-powerful central government.

At Gunston Hall on Sunday, September 30, Jefferson

listened intently to the opinions, advice, and reminiscences of his old friend: the national debt, paper currency, taxes, the Constitutional Convention with its shameful bargain that permitted twenty more years of the slave trade. Jefferson made copious notes, which he preserved and which still exist.

An entry in the Gunston Hall Bible records that Mason was buried in the family graveyard on the estate he owned and loved.

Gunston Hall still stands, much as it was in the days of George Mason. As a national memorial it is not as imposing as George Washington's Mount Vernon or Thomas Jefferson's Monticello, visited annually by thousands of tourists. Rather it is a reminder of the love that a man of great wisdom, concern, and ability had for the home he lived in most of his life. George Mason's real memorial is in the enduring words of the Bill of Rights, which intimately touches the lives of all Americans every day.

APPENDIX

FINAL DRAFT OF THE VIRGINIA DECLARATION OF RIGHTS

[12 June 1776]

A DECLARATION OF RIGHTS made by the Representatives of the good people of VIRGINIA, assembled in full and free Convention; which rights do pertain to (them and their) posterity, as the basis and foundation of Government.

1. That all men are (by nature) equally free and independent, and have certain inherent rights, of which, (when they enter into a state of society,) they cannot, by any compact, deprive or divest their posterity; (namely,) the enjoyment of life and liberty, with the means of acquiring and possessing property, and pursuing and obtaining happiness and safety.

2. That all power is vested in, and consequently derived from, the People; that magistrates are their trustees and servants, and at all times amenable to them.

[*157*]

3. That Government is, or ought to be, instituted for the common benefit, protection, and security of the people, nation, or community;— of all the various modes and forms of Government that is best which is capable of producing the greatest degree of happiness and safety, and is most effectually secured against the danger of mal-administration;— and that, whenever any Government shall be found inadequate or contrary to these purposes, a majority of the community hath an indubitable, unalienable, and indefeasible right, to reform, alter, or abolish it, in such manner as shall be judged most conducive to the publick weal.

4. That no man, or set of men, are entitled to exclusive or separate emoluments and privileges from the community, but in consideration of publick services; which, not being descendible, (neither ought the offices) of Magistrate, Legislator, or Judge, (to be hereditary).

5. That the Legislative and Executive powers of the State should be separate and distinct from the Judicative; and, that the members of the two first may be restrained from oppression, by feeling and participating the burdens of the people, they should, at fixed periods, be reduced to a private station, return into that body from which they were originally taken, and the vacancies be supplied by frequent, certain, and regular elections, (in which all, or any part of the former members, to be again eligible, or ineligible, as the law shall direct).

6. That elections of members to serve as Representatives of the people, in Assembly, ought to be free; and that all men, having sufficient evidence of permanent common interest with, and attachment to, the community, have the right of suffrage, (and cannot be taxed or deprived of their property for) publick uses without their own consent or that of their Representative (so elected,) nor bound by any law to which they have not, in like manner, assented, for the publick good.

7. That all power of suspending laws, or the execution of laws, by any authority, without consent of the Representatives of the people, is injurious to their rights, and ought not to be exercised.

8. That in all capital or criminal prosecutions a man hath a right to demand the cause and nature of his accusation, to be confronted with the accusers and witnesses, to call for evidence in his favour, and to a speedy trial by an impartial jury of his vicinage, without whose unanimous consent he cannot be found guilty, nor can he be compelled to give

evidence against himself; that no man be deprived of his liberty except by the law of the land, or the judgment of his peers.

9. That excessive bail ought not to be required, nor excessive fines imposed, nor cruel and unusual punishments inflicted.

10. That (general) warrants, whereby any officer or messenger may be commanded to search suspected places (without evidence of a fact committed,) or to seize any person or persons (not named, or whose offence is) not particularly described (and supported by evidence,) are grievous and oppressive, and ought not to be granted.

11. That in controversies respecting property, and in suits between man and man, the ancient trial by Jury is preferable to any other, and ought to be held sacred.

12. That the freedom of the Press is one of the greatest bulwarks of liberty, and can never be restrained but by despotick Governments.

13. That a well-regulated Militia, composed of the body of the people, trained to arms, is the proper, natural, and safe defence of a free State; that Standing Armies, in time of peace, should be avoided as dangerous to liberty; and that, in all cases, the military should be under strict subordination to, and governed by, the civil power.

14. That the people have a right to uniform Government; and, therefore, that no Government separate from, or independent of, the Government of *Virginia*, ought to be erected or established within the limits thereof.

15. That no free Government, or the blessing of liberty, can be preserved to any people but by a firm adherence to justice, moderation, temperance, frugality, and virtue, and by frequent recurrence to fundamental principles.

16. That Religion, or the duty which we owe to our *Creator,* and the manner of discharging it, can be directed only by reason and conviction, not by force or violence; and, therefore, all men (are equally entitled to the free) exercise of religion, according to the dictates of conscience; and that it is the mutual duty of all to practise Christian forbearance, love, and charity, towards each other.

INDEX

JAMES AYARS was born in a suburb of Chicago but spent his youth on a farm between Paw Paw and Kalamazoo, Michigan. After graduation from Northwestern University he became a high school teacher and later an editor of scientific bulletins.

He has written a number of books for children and young people and collaborated with his wife on one, *Contrary Jenkins*. His *The Illinois River* received the Clara Ingram Judson award of the Society of Midland Authors in 1969.

To do research for *We Hold These Truths*, Mr. Ayars went to England, where he visited Stephen Langton's Canterbury, John Lilburne's London, and Runnymede, where the barons presented King John with Magna Carta.

James Ayars and his wife, Rebecca Caudill, a well-known author of children's books, live in Urbana, Illinois.